# The History of King Richard III

(unfinished) written by Master Thomas More,
then one of the undersheriffs of London,
about the year of Our Lord 1513. Which work has been
before this time printed in Harding's Chronicle, and
in Hall's Chronicle[1], but very much corrupt in
many places, sometime having less, and sometime
having more, and altered in words and whole
sentences; much varying from the copy
of his own hand, by which
this is printed.[2]

## Sir Thomas More

ET REMOTISSIMA PROPE

Hesperus Classics

Hesperus Classics
Published by Hesperus Press Limited
4 Rickett Street, London sw6 1RU
www.hesperuspress.com

First published in 1557
First published by Hesperus Press Limited, 2005

Foreword © Sister Wendy Beckett, 2005

Designed and typeset by Fraser Muggeridge
Printed in Italy by Graphic Studio Srl

ISBN: 1-84391-107-8

# CONTENTS

The first time I saw a photograph of a saint I caught my breath in wonder. It was of St Therese of Lisieux, a young nun who died at the end of the nineteenth century and, fortunately for us, had been much photographed by her elder sister. To see for myself, as it were, the actual face of one who had loved God so passionately, brought me very close to tears. Painting cannot have the same impact. Sometimes it is likely that the artist had, in fact, seen the saint: how else would he know that St Charles Borromeo had that immense jut of a nose, dwarfing his other features into insignificance? Equally, we can guess that no artist who painted St Thomas Aquinas had seen him in the all-too-solid flesh – flesh so superabundant that a circle had to be cut in the refectory table so he could reach his plate. The depicted St Thomas has the austere lineaments of the artist's innocent expectations. But here, as in many other ways, St Thomas More had remarkable fortune. His dear friend Erasmus, the most famous scholar in Europe, had as a friend Holbein, the most famous painter, especially the most famous portraitist. Thomas More's own good friend, Henry VIII, the most famous monarch, naturally wanted Holbein for his Court artist, which has given us a splendid array of Tudor likenesses on which to ponder. Holbein, of course, was a Court artist and his aim was not only to represent but to please. Being a rare genius, he managed as a rule to show his sitter what he or she wanted to see and also to show the viewer what Holbein saw and wanted us to see. His portrait of Henry has all the overwhelming sense of authority that this megalomaniac wanted: Henry looms out at us, overflowing the bounds of the frame, terrifying, majestic, dense with charisma. But Holbein faithfully shows us, too, those small piggy eyes and the brutality of the mean, pursed mouth. Yet when we turn to Holbein on More we may be surprised.

Thomas More was one of the most renowned of wits, a scholar almost on the level of Erasmus, a man admired from youth – or so his son-in-law assures us – as very close to God. He was universally popular. Even the scholars he excoriated in true Renaissance style seem to have appreciated if not his criticism, then at least the brilliance of its expression. (Perhaps only the poor religious dissidents whom he righteously persecuted as infested with spiritual disease and contagious to others, disliked him, as – in this one instance – do we.) But Holbein does not show us a merry Thomas, despite 'merry' being one of his favourite words, nor even a witty Thomas, far less a saintly Thomas. He shows us, instead, the dignity of Thomas the Lord Chancellor – a strong, rather melancholy man, eminently judicious, quiet, inward-looking, but not, it would seem, all that content with what he sees there. (If Thomas saw his heresy-pursuing we would be pleased for him to look remorseful, but that horrid activity he saw, alas, as a sacred duty.) Maybe Holbein is hinting at the saint's humility.

His writings, too, give little indication of holiness. The exception is the volume of his letters from prison, beautiful letters, radiant with a quiet faith and a determination to choose God above earthly happiness and life itself. If ever a martyr faced death deliberately and with a certainty of duty, un-clouded by emotion, unsupported by fellow-believers, that was St Thomas More. But his famous *Utopia* is a book more known for its title than its content and seems all too often bafflingly ambivalent. What then of this 'history' which he wrote in his relative youth.

Of all his works this is the hardest to reconcile with sanctity. So much so that admirers have tried to insist that the actual author was his early patron, Archbishop Morton, and Thomas merely the scribe. This theory has also appealed to those eager to defend Richard III from its devastating strictures. Modern scholarship has settled the matter: this is a book by Thomas More. Yet it is hardly a book, and certainly not a history of Richard III, unhappy man. It hones in on the last two or three years of Richard's life, and even then, only on that portion when he made his bid for power. What happened before, and even what happened after – the bloody tragedy of Bosworth – does not interest the author. It is clear where his interest lies: in the lure of power, and the intellectual and moral extremes to which a man will go in search of it. Erasmus said of Thomas More that he 'always had a peculiar loathing for tyranny', but I think More saw a natural desire for power in each of us and one that would inevitably, given scope, develop into tyranny. He longed ardently for freedom, for himself and others – above all freedom to do what was right. Richard, he thought, was a prime example of a man who manipulated, ignored conscience, twisted the laws of both God and man, and in the end found himself the pitiable and haunted figure that More describes so memorably. It is a remarkably vivid account, almost a novel in its immediacy and intimacy. More enters into every convolution of the plot, every emotion of the players. Here is a born raconteur, almost convincing us that he has been there and seen for himself and now shares with us his insights. No wonder that when Shakespeare came to read it, he set to and produced that vigorous drama that has formed for ever the national mind on what to make of this short-lived reign.

A brilliant book, indeed, and a compelling read: but the work of a saint? More is harsh in his judgements: who can forget the relish with which he describes the evil fates that lay in wait for the traitorous villains like Dr Shaa or Miles Forest or Richard himself, bedraggled in death with his hair wild 'like a cur-dog'? It can come across as a vindictive book, a winner's version of the loser's actions, and it is this element of quiet ferocity that disturbs. Why did he write it? It was never published in his lifetime, and never even finished. Did he begin to think – man of virtue as he undoubtedly was – that it did indeed sound like party politics? He had clearly felt the need to involve himself emotionally in this great dynastic turning point that had affected so many of his older contemporaries, his friend Bishop Morton among them. Was it an abstract interest? Or, as seems to me much more likely, was More really writing this for himself? Was he acting out, harmlessly, the causes and results of ambition? Was it a healthy catharsis, almost a private act of personal purification? And was his mistake that of genius, achieving this end with such power that the whole world wants to read what he wrote and enter into its flow? Over twenty years of political activity and spiritual development lay ahead of him: did he exorcise his ambition and control his temptations in this wonderful book?

– *Sister Wendy Beckett, 2005*

In 1557 William Rastell, the nephew and publisher of Sir Thomas More, wrote a pithy commentary on the short publication history of *The History of King Richard III*, saying that the text was written around 1513 and 'has been before this time printed in Harding's *Chronicle*, and in Hall's *Chronicle*, but very much corrupt in many places, sometime having less, and sometime having more, and altered in words and whole sentences; much varying from the copy of his own hand...' The chronicles that he mentions were rather dull and (as one might expect from their titles) chronological records of events, but as well as recording history such chronicles tended to subvert it towards the compiler's own ideology. Rastell did readers a great service in rescuing More's original text from the unreliable and partisan editing of those previous publications. However, it was no easy job for him. That original text existed in two versions, as the *History of Richard III*, and as the Latin version *Historia Richardi Tertius*. It seems More wrote both versions at much the same time, and although they are closely connected, inevitably there are also differences. There are episodes that are treated in a fuller way in the Latin version than in the English version; Rastell translated these episodes into English and inserted them into his edition. Modern editions, including this one, tend to retain the fruits of his labours. In this edition also the spelling and punctuation have been freely modernised, and a glossary is provided for words that are archaic or that have since changed in meaning.

# The History of
# King Richard III

King Edward, of that name the Fourth, after that he had lived fifty-three years, seven months, and six days[3], and thereof reigned twenty-two years, one month, and eight days, died at Westminster the ninth day of April, the year of our redemption 1483, leaving much fair issue, that is to wit: Edward[4], the Prince, at thirteen years of age; Richard[5], Duke of York, two years younger; Elizabeth[6], whose fortune and grace was after to be Queen, wife to King Henry the Seventh, and mother to the Eighth; Cecily[7], not so fortunate as fair; Bridget[8], which, representing the virtue of her whose name she bore, professed and observed a religious life in Dartford, a house of close nuns; Anne[9], that was after honourably married to Thomas, then Lord Howard and after Earl of Surrey; and Katherine[10], which long time tossed in either fortune, sometimes in wealth, often in adversity at the last – if this be the last, for yet she lives, is by the benignity of her nephew, King Henry the Eighth, in very prosperous estate and worthy her birth and virtue.

This noble Prince deceased at his Palace of Westminster, and with great funeral honour and heaviness of his people, from thence conveyed, was interred at Windsor. A king of such governance and behaviour in time of peace (for in war each party must needs be the other's enemy), that there was never any prince of this land attaining the Crown by battle so heartily beloved with the substance of the people; nor he himself so specially in any part of his life as at the time of his death. Which favour and affection, yet after his decease, by the cruelty, mischief, and trouble of the tempestuous world that followed, highly towards him more increased. At such time as he died, the displeasure of those that bore him grudges – for King Henry's sake (the Sixth), whom he deposed[11] – was well assuaged, and in effect quenched, in that many of them were dead in more than twenty years of his reign, a great part of

3

a long life. And many of them in the mean season grown into his favour, of which he was never strange. He was a goodly personage, and very princely to behold, of heart courageous, politic in counsel, in adversity nothing abashed, in prosperity rather joyful than proud, in peace just and merciful, in war sharp and fierce, in the field bold and hardy, and nevertheless – no further than wisdom would – adventurous. Whose wars who so well consider, he shall no less command his wisdom where he voided, than his manhood where he vanquished.

He was of visage lovely, of body mighty, strong, and clean made, howbeit in his latter days with over-liberal diet somewhat corpulent and burly, and nevertheless not uncomely; he was of youth greatly given to fleshly wantonness, from which health of body in great prosperity and fortune, without a special grace, hardly refrains. This fault not greatly grieved the people, for neither could any one man's pleasure stretch and extend to the displeasure of very many, and was without violence, and, over that, in his latter days lessened and well left.

In which time of his later days, this realm was in quiet and prosperous estate: no fear of outward enemies, no war in hand, nor none toward but such as no man looked for; the people towards the Prince not in a constrained fear, but in a willing and loving obedience; among themselves, the commons in good peace. The lords whom he knew at variance, himself in his deathbed appeased. He had left all gathering of money (which is the only thing that withdraws the hearts of Englishmen from the Prince)[12], nor anything intended he to take in hand, by which he should be driven thereto, for his tribute[13] out of France he had before obtained. And the year foregoing his death, he had obtained Berwick[14]. And albeit that all the time of his reign, he was with his people, so benign,

4

courteous and so familiar that no part of his virtues was more esteemed; yet that condition in the end of his days (in which many princes by a long continued sovereignty decline in to a proud port, from debonair behaviour of their beginning) marvellously in him grew and increased; so far forth that in the summer the last that ever he saw, His Highness, being at Windsor in hunting, sent for the Mayor and aldermen of London to him, for no other errand but to have them hunt and be merry with him; where he made them not so stately, but so friendly and so familiar cheer, and sent venison from thence so freely into the city that no one thing in many days before got him either more hearts or more hearty favour among the common people, which oftentimes more esteem and take for greater kindness, a little courtesy, than a great benefit.

So deceased (as I have said) this noble King, in that time in which his life was most desired. Whose love of his people and their entire affection towards him had been to his noble children (having in themselves also as many gifts of nature, as many princely virtues, as much goodly towardness as their age could receive) a marvellous fortress and sure armour – if division and dissension of their friends had not unarmed them, and left them destitute, and the execrable desire of sovereignty provoked him to their destruction, which if either kinship or kindness had held place, must needs have been their chief defence. For Richard, the Duke of Gloucester[15], by nature their uncle, by office their Protector, to their father beholden, to themselves by oath and allegiance bound, all the bands broke that bind man and man together; without any respect of God or the world, unnaturally contrived to bereave them, not only their dignity, but also their lives. But forasmuch as this Duke's demeanour ministers in effect all the whole matter whereof this book shall entreat, it is therefore convenient, somewhat, to show you before we further go, what manner of man this was, that could find in his heart so much mischief to conceive.

Richard[16], Duke of York, a noble man and a mighty, began not by war, but by law, to challenge the Crown, putting his claim into the Parliament; where his cause was either for right or favour so far forth advanced, that King Henry his blood (albeit he had a goodly prince) utterly rejected, the Crown was by authority of Parliament entailed to the Duke of York and his issue male in remainder, immediately after the death of King Henry. But the Duke not enduring so long to tarry, but intending under pretext of dissension and debate arising in the realm to prevent his time, and take upon him the rule in King Harry his life, was with many nobles of the realm at Wakefield[17] slain, leaving three sons: Edward, George, and Richard. All three, as they were great states of birth, so were they great and stately of stomach, greedy and ambitious of authority, and impatient of partners.

Edward, revenging his father's death, deprived King Henry and attained the Crown.

George, Duke of Clarence, was a goodly noble prince, and at all points fortunate, if either his own ambition had not set him against his brother, or the envy of his enemies his brother against him. For were it by the Queen[18] and the lords of her blood, which highly maligned the King's kindred (as women commonly not of malice but of nature hate them whom their husbands love); or were it a proud appetite of the Duke himself intending to be king; at the leastwise, heinous treason was there laid to his charge[19], and finally, were he faulty, were he faultless, attainted was he by Parliament, and judged to the death, and thereupon hastily drowned in a butt of malmsey; whose death King Edward (albeit he commanded it) when he wist it was done, piteously bewailed and sorrowfully repented.

Richard, the third son, of whom we now entreat, was in wit and courage equal with either of them, in body and prowess far under them both; little of stature, ill-featured of limbs, crook-backed, his left shoulder much higher than his right, hard-favoured of visage, and such as is in states called warlike, in other men otherwise. He was malicious, wrathful, envious, and from afore his birth ever froward. It is for truth reported that the Duchess his mother had so much ado in her travail that she could not be delivered of him uncut; and that he came into the world with the feet forward, as men be born outward, and (as the fame runs) also not untoothed – whether men of hatred report about the truth, or else that nature changed her course in his beginning, which in the course of his life many things unnaturally committed. No evil captain was he in the war, as to which his disposition was more meetly than for peace. Sundry victories had he, and sometime overthrows, but never in default as for his own person, either of hardiness or politic order. Free was he called of dispense, and somewhat above his power liberal; with large gifts he got him unsteadfast friendship, for which he was fain to pill and spoil in other places and get him steadfast hatred. He was close and secret, a deep dissimuler, lowly of countenance, arrogant of heart, outwardly coumpinable where he inwardly hated, not letting to kiss whom he thought to kill; dispiteous and cruel, not for evil will always, but after for ambition, and either for the surety or increase of his estate. Friend and foe was much what indifferent; where his advantage grew, he spared no man death whose life withstood his purpose. He slew with his own hands King Henry the Sixth, being prisoner in the Tower, as men constantly say – and that without commandment or knowledge of the King, which would undoubtedly, if he had intended that thing, have appointed that butcherly office to some other than his own born brother. Some wise men also ween that his drift, covertly conveyed, lacked not in helping forth his brother of Clarence to his death; which he resisted openly, howbeit somewhat (as men deemed) more faintly than he that were heartily minded to his wealth. And they that thus deem, think that he long time in King Edward's life forethought to be king, in case that the King his brother (whose life he looked that evil diet should shorten) should happen to decease (as indeed he did) while his children were young. And they deem that for this intent he was glad of his brother's death, that Duke of Clarence, whose life must needs have hindered him so intending; whether the same Duke of Clarence had he kept him true to his nephew, the young King, or enterprised to be king himself.

But of all this point is there no certainty, and whoso divines upon conjectures may as well shoot too far as too short. Howbeit, this have I by credible information learnt, that the self night in which King Edward died, one Mistlebrook, long before morning, came in great haste to the house of one Potter, dwelling in Redcross Street without Cripplegate;[20] and when he was with hasty rapping quickly let in, he showed to Potter that King Edward was departed. 'By my troth man,' quod Potter, 'then will my master the Duke of Gloucester be king.' What cause he had so to think, hard it is to say – whether, he being towards him, anything knew that he such thing purposed, or otherwise had any inkling thereof; for he was not likely to speak it of nought.

But now to return to the course of this history. Were it that the Duke of Gloucester had of old foreminded this conclusion, or was now at erst thereunto moved, and put in hope by the occasion of the tender age of the young Princes his nephews – as opportunity and likelihood of speed puts a man in courage of that he never intended – certain is it that he contrived their destruction, with the usurpation of the regal dignity upon himself. And forasmuch as he well wist and helped to maintain a long continued grudge and heart brenning between the Queen's kindred and the King's blood, either party envying other's authority, he now thought that their division should be (as it was indeed) a fortherly beginning to the pursuit of his intent and a sure ground for the foundation of all his building, if he might first, under the pretext of revenging of old displeasure, abuse the anger and ignorance of the one party to the destruction of the other, and then win to his purpose as many as he could; and those that could not be won might be lost before they looked therefore. For of one thing was he certain; that if his intent were perceived, he should soon have made peace between the both parties with his own blood.

King Edward in his life, albeit that this dissension between his friends somewhat irked him, yet in his good health he somewhat the less regarded it because he thought whatsoever business should fall between them, himself should always be able to rule both the parties. But in his last sickness, when he perceived his natural strength so sore enfeebled that he despaired all recovery, then he, considering the youth of his children – albeit he nothing less mistrusted than that which happened, yet well foreseeing that many harms might grow by their debate while the youth of his children should lack discretion of themselves and good counsel of their friends, of which either party should counsel for their own commodity

9

and rather by pleasant advice to win themselves favour, than by profitable advertisement to do the children good – he called some of them before him that were at variance, and in especial the Lord Marquis Dorset[21], the Queen's son by her first husband, and Richard the Lord Hastings[22], a noble man, then Lord Chamberlain, against whom the Queen specially grudged for the great favour the King bore him, and also for that she thought him secretly familiar with the King in wanton company. Her kindred also bore him sore, as well for that the King had made him Captain of Calais (which office the Lord Rivers[23], brother to the Queen, claimed of the King's former promise), as for divers other great gifts which he received that they looked for.

When these lords with divers other of both the parties were come in presence, the King, lifting up himself and underset with pillows, as it is reported, on this wise said to them:

'My Lords, my dear kinsmen and allies, in what plight I lie you see, and I feel. By which, the less while I look to live with you, the more deeply am I moved to care in what case I leave you; for such as I leave you, such be my children like to find you. Which if they should (that God forbid) find you at variance, might hap to fall themselves at war before their discretion would serve to set you at peace. You see their youth, of which I reckon the only surety to rest in your concord. For it suffices not that all you love them, if each of you hate other. If they were men, your faithfulness haply would suffice. But childhood must be maintained by men's authority, and slipper youth underpropped with older counsel, which neither they can have but you give it, nor you give it if you agree not. For where each labours to break that the other makes, and for hatred of each other's person impugn each other's counsel, there must it needs be long before any good conclusion go forward. And also while either party labours to be chief, flattery shall have more place than plain and faithful advice, of which must needs ensue the evil bringing up of the Prince, whose mind in tender youth infected, shall readily fall to mischief and riot, and draw down with this noble realm to ruin; but if grace turn him to wisdom, which if God send, then they that by evil means before pleased him best, shall after fall furthest out of favour, so that ever at length evil drifts drive to nought and good plain ways prosper. Great variance has there long been between you, not always for great causes. Sometimes a thing right well intended, our misconstruction turns to worse, or a small displeasure done us, either our own affection or evil tongues aggrieve.

'But this wot I well: you never had so great cause of hatred, as you have of love. That we be all men, that we be Christian men, this shall I leave for preachers to tell you (and yet I wot never whether any preacher's words ought more to move you than his that is by and by going to the place that they all preach of). But this shall I desire you to remember, that the one part of you is of my blood, the other of mine allies, and each of you with other, either of kindred or affinity; which spiritual kindred of affinity, if the sacraments of Christ's Church bear that weight with us that would God they did, should no less move us to charity, than the respect of fleshly consanguinity. Our Lord forbid that you love together the worse, for the self cause that you ought to love the better. And yet that happens. And no where find we so deadly debate, as among them which by nature and law most ought to agree together. Such a pestilent serpent is ambition and desire of vainglory and sovereignty, which among states where he once enters creeps forth so far, till with division and variance he turns all to mischief – first longing to be next the best, afterward equal with the best, and at last chief and above the best. Of which immoderate appetite of worship, and thereby of debate and dissension, what loss, what sorrow, what trouble has within these few years grown in this realm, I pray God as well forget as we well remember. Which things if I could as well have foreseen, as I have with my more pain than pleasure proved, by God's blessed lady (that was ever his oath) I would never have won the courtesy of men's knees with the loss of so many heads.

'But since things past cannot be gaincalled, much ought we the more beware, by what occasion we have taken so great hurt afore, that we eftsoons fall not in that occasion again. Now be those griefs passed, and all is (God be thanked) quiet, and likely right well to prosper in wealthful peace under your cousins my children, if God send them life and you love. Of which two things, the less loss were they by whom though God did his pleasure, yet should the realm always find kings and peradventure as good kings. But if you among yourselves in a child's reign fall at debate, many a good man shall perish and haply he too, and you too, before this land find peace again. Wherefore, in these last words that ever I look to speak with you: I exhort you and require you all, for the love that I have ever born to you, for the love that our Lord bears to us all, from this time forward, all grieves forgotten, each of you love other. Which I verily trust you will, if you anything earthly regard – either God or your King, affinity or kindred, this realm, your own country, or your own surety.'

And therewithal the King no longer enduring to sit up, laid him down on his right side, his face towards them; and none was there present that could refrain from weeping. But the lords recomforting him with as good words as they could and answering, for the time, as they thought to stand with his pleasure, there in his presence (as by their words appeared) each forgave other and joined their hands together, when (as it after appeared by their deeds) their hearts were far asunder.

As soon as the King was departed, that noble Prince, his son, drew towards London, which, at the time of his decease, kept his household at Ludlow in Wales. Which country, being far off from the law and recourse to justice, was begun to be far out of goodwill and waxen wild, robbers and reivers walking at liberty uncorrected. And for this encheason the Prince was in the life of his father sent thither, to the end that the authority of his presence should refrain evil-disposed persons from the boldness of their former outrages. To the governance and ordering of this young Prince, at his sending thither, was there appointed Sir Anthony Woodville, Lord Rivers and brother to the Queen, a right honourable man, as valiant of hand as politic in counsel. Adjoined were there to him other of the same party, and, in effect, every one as he was nearest of kin to the Queen, so was planted next about the Prince.

That drift, by the Queen not unwisely devised, whereby her blood might of youth be rooted in the Prince's favour, the Duke of Gloucester turned to their destruction, and upon that ground set the foundation of all his unhappy building. For whomsoever he perceived either at variance with them or bearing himself their favour, he broke to them – some by mouth, some by writing and secret messengers – that it neither was reason nor in any wise to be suffered that the young King, their master and kinsman, should be in the hands and custody of his mother's kindred, sequestered in manner from their company and attendance, of which everyone ought him as faithful service as they, and many of them far more honourable part of kin than his mother's side; 'Whose blood,' quod he, 'saving the King's pleasure, was full unmeetly to be matched with his; which now to be, as who say removed from the King and the less noble to be left about him, is,' quod he, 'neither honourable to His Majesty nor to us, and also to his grace no surety to have the mightiest of his friends from him, and to us no little jeopardy to suffer our well-proved evil-willers to grow in over-great authority with the Prince in youth, namely which is light of belief and soon persuaded.

'You remember, I trow, King Edward himself, albeit he was a man of age and of discretion, yet was he in many things ruled by the bend, more than stood either with his honour or our profit, or with the commodity of any man else, except only the immoderate advancement of themselves. Which whether they sorer thirsted after their own weal, or our woe, it were hard, I ween, to guess. And if some folk's friendship had not held better place with the King than any respect of kindred, they might peradventure easily have betrapped and brought to confusion some of us before this. Why not as easily as they have done some other already, as near of his royal blood as we? But our Lord has wrought his will, and thanks be to his grace that peril is past. Howbeit, as great is growing if we suffer this young King in our enemy's hand, which without his witting might abuse the name of his commandment to any of our undoing, which thing God and good provision forbid. Of which good provision none of us has anything the less need for the late-made atonement in which the King's pleasure had more place than the parties' wills. Nor none of us, I believe, is so unwise, oversoon to trust a new friend made of an old foe, or to think that an hoverly kindness, suddenly contracted in one hour, continued yet scant a fortnight, should be deeper settled in their stomachs than a long accustomed malice many years rooted.'

With these words and writings and such other, the Duke of Gloucester soon set a-fire them that were of themselves easy to kindle, and in especial twain, Edward, Duke of Buckingham[24], and Richard, Lord Hastings and chamberlain, both men of honour and of great power – the one by long succession from his ancestry, the other by his office and the King's favour. These two, not bearing each to other so much love as hatred, both to the Queen's party, in this point accorded together with the Duke of Gloucester that they would utterly amove from the King's company all his mother's friends, under the name of their enemies.

Upon this concluded, the Duke of Gloucester, understanding that the lords which at that time were about the King intended to bring him up to his coronation, accompanied with such power of their friends that it should be hard for him to bring his purpose to pass without the gathering and great assembling of people, and in manner of open war, whereof the end he wist was doubtous, and in which the King being on their side, his part should have the face and name of a rebellion; he secretly therefore by divers means caused the Queen to be persuaded, and brought in the mind that it neither were needed, and also should be jeopardous, the King to come up strong. For where as now every lord loved other, and no other thing studied upon but about the coronation and honour of the King; if the lords of her kindred should assemble in the King's name much people, they should give the lords atwixt whom and them had been sometime debate, to fear and suspect, lest they should gather this people not for the King's safeguard whom no man impugned, but for their destruction, having more regard to their old variance than their new atonement. For which cause they should assemble on the other party much people again for their defence, whose power she wist well far stretched. And thus should all the realm fall on a roar. And of all the hurt that thereof should ensue, which was likely not to be little, and the most harm there like to fall where she least would, all the world would put her and her kindred in the wight and say that they had unwisely, and untruly also, broken the amity and peace that the King, her husband, so prudently made between his kin and hers in his deathbed, and which the other party faithfully observed.

The Queen, being in this wise persuaded, such word sent to her son[25] and to her brother[26], being about the King; and over that the Duke of Gloucester himself and other lords, the chief of his bend, wrote to the King so reverently, and to the Queen's friends there so lovingly, that they – nothing earthly mistrusting – brought the King up in great haste, not in good speed, with a sober company.

Now was the King in his way to London gone, from Northampton, when these Dukes of Gloucester and Buckingham came thither. Where remained behind the Lord Rivers, the King's uncle, intending on the morrow to follow the King and be with him at Stony Stratford, eleven miles thence, early before he departed. So was there made that night much friendly cheer between these Dukes and the Lord Rivers a great while. But incontinent after that they were openly with great courtesy departed, and the Lord Rivers lodged, the Dukes – secretly with a few of their most privy friends – set them down in council, wherein they spent a great part of the night. And at their rising in the dawning of the day, they sent about privily to their servants in their inns and lodgings about, giving the commandment to make themselves shortly ready, for their lords were to horsebackward. Upon which messages many of their folk were attendant, when many of the Lord River's servants were unready. Now had these Dukes taken also into their custody the keys of the inn, that none should pass forth without their licence. And over this, in the highway towards Stony Stratford where the King lay, they had bestowed certain of their folk that should send back again and compel to return any man that were gotten out of Northampton towards Stony Stratford, till they should give other licence; forasmuch as the Dukes themselves intended, for the show of their diligence, to be the first that should that day attend upon the King's Highness out of that town – thus bore they folk in hand[27].

But when the Lord Rivers understood the gates closed, and the ways on every side beset, neither his servants nor himself suffered to go out, perceiving well so great a thing without his knowledge not begun for nought, comparing this manner present with this last night's cheer, in so few hours so great a change marvellously misliked. Howbeit, since he could not get away – and keep himself close he would not, lest he should seem to hide himself for some secret fear of his own fault, whereof he saw no such cause in himself – he determined upon the surety of his own conscience, to go boldly to them and enquire what this matter might mean. Whom as soon as they saw, they began to quarrel with him and say that he intended to set distance between the King and them and to bring them to confusion, but it should not lie in his power. And when he began (as he was a very well spoken man) in goodly wise to excuse himself, they tarried not the end of his answer, but shortly took him and put him in ward; and that done, forthwith went to horseback and took the way to Stony Stratford, where they found the King with his company ready to leap on horseback and depart forward, to leave that lodging for them because it was too strait for both companies.

And as soon as they came in his presence, they light adown with all their company about them. To whom the Duke of Buckingham said, 'Go afore, gentlemen and yeomen, keep your rooms.' And thus in a goodly array they came to the King, and on their knees in very humble wise saluted His Grace; which received them in very joyous and amiable manner, nothing earthly knowing nor mistrusting as yet. But even by and by in his presence, they picked a quarrel to the Lord Richard Grey, the King's other brother by his mother, saying that he, with the Lord Marquis his brother and the Lord Rivers his uncle, had compassed to rule the King and the realm and to set variance among the states, and to subdue and destroy the noble blood of the realm. Towards the accomplishing whereof, they said that the Lord Marquis had entered into the Tower of London and thence taken out the King's Treasure, and sent men to the sea. All which thing these Dukes wist well were done for good purposes and necessary by the whole council at London, saving that somewhat they must say. To which words the King answered, 'What my brother Marquis has done I cannot say. But in good faith I dare well answer for mine uncle Rivers and my brother here, that they be innocent of any such matters.'

'Yea, My Liege,' quod the Duke of Buckingham, 'they have kept their dealing in these matters far from the knowledge of your good grace.' And forthwith they arrested the Lord Richard and Sir Thomas Vaughan[28], knight, in the King's presence, and brought the King and all back to Northampton, where they took again further counsel. And there they sent away from the King whom it pleased them, and set new servants about him such as liked them better than him. At which dealing he wept and was nothing content, but it booted not. And at dinner the Duke of

Gloucester sent a dish from his own table to the Lord Rivers, praying him to be of good cheer, all should be well enough. And he thanked the Duke, and prayed the messenger to bear it to his nephew, the Lord Richard, with the same message for his comfort, who he thought had more need of comfort, as one to whom such adversity was strange. But himself had been all his days in ure therewith, and therefore could bear it the better. But for all this comfortable courtesy of the Duke of Gloucester he sent the Lord Rivers and the Lord Richard with Sir Thomas Vaughan into the north country into divers places to prison, and afterward all to Pomfret[29], where they were in conclusion beheaded.

In this wise the Duke of Gloucester took upon himself the order and governance of the young King, whom with much honour and humble reverence he conveyed upward towards the city. But anon the tidings of this matter came hastily to the Queen, a little before the midnight following, and that in the sorest wise: that the King, her son, was taken; her brother, her son and her other friends arrested and sent no man wist whither, to be done with God wot what. With which tidings the Queen in great fright and heaviness, bewailing her child's ruin, her friends' mischance, and her own infortune, damning the time that ever she dissuaded the gathering of power about the King, got herself in all the haste possible with her younger son and her daughters out of the Palace of Westminster in which she then lay, into the sanctuary[30], lodging herself and her company there in the Abbot's place.

Now came there in one likewise not long after midnight, from the Lord Chamberlain to the Archbishop of York[31], then Chancellor of England, to his place not far from Westminster. And for that he showed his servants that he had tidings of so great importance that his master gave him in charge not to forbear his rest, they letted not to wake him, nor he to admit this messenger in to his bedside. Of whom he heard that these Dukes were gone back with the King's grace from Stony Stratford to Northampton. 'Notwithstanding, sir,' quod he, 'My Lord sends Your Lordship word that there is no fear, for he assures you that all shall be well.'

'I assure him,' quod the Archbishop, 'be it as well as it will, it will never be so well as we have seen it.' And thereupon, by and by after the messenger departed, he caused in all the haste all his servants to be called up, and so with his own household about him and every man weaponed, he took the great seal[32] with him and came yet before day to the Queen. About whom he found much heaviness, rumble, haste and business, carriage and conveyance of her stuff into sanctuary – chests, coffers, packs, fardels, trusses, all on men's backs, no man unoccupied; some loading, some going, some discharging, some coming for more, some breaking down the walls to bring in the next way, and some yet drew to them that helped to carry a wrong way. The Queen herself sat alone alow on the rushes, all desolate and dismayed, whom the Archbishop comforted in the best manner he could, showing her that he trusted the matter was nothing so sore as she took it for; and that he was put in good hope and out of fear by the message sent him from the Lord Chamberlain.

'Ah woe worth him,' quod she, 'for he is one of them that labours to destroy me and my blood.'

'Madam,' quod he, 'be you of good cheer. For I assure you if they crown any other king than your son, whom they now have with them, we shall on the morrow crown his brother whom you have here with you. And here is the great seal, which in likewise as that noble Prince your husband delivered it to me, so here I deliver it to you, to the use and behoof of your son,' and therewith he betook her the great seal, and departed home again, yet in the dawning of the day. By which time he might in his chamber window see all the Thames full of boats of the Duke of Gloucester's servants, watching that no man should go to sanctuary, nor none could pass unsearched.

Then was there great commotion and murmur as well in other places about, as specially in the city, the people diversely divining upon this dealing. And some lords, knights and gentlemen, either for favour of the Queen or for fear of themselves, assembled in sundry companies and went flockmeal in harness, and many also for that they reckoned this demeanour attempted not so specially against the other lords, as against the King himself in the disturbance of his coronation.

But then by and by the lords assembled together at London. Towards which meeting, the Archbishop of York, fearing that it would be ascribed (as it was indeed) to his overmuch lightness that he so suddenly had yielded up the great seal to the Queen, to whom the custody thereof nothing pertained without especial commandment of the King, secretly sent for the seal again and brought it with him after the customable manner. And at this meeting the Lord Hastings, whose troth towards the King no man doubted nor needed to doubt, persuaded the lords to believe that the Duke of Gloucester was sure and fastly faithful to his Prince and that the Lord Rivers and Lord Richard, with the other knights, were – for matters attempted by them against the Dukes of Gloucester and Buckingham – put under arrest for their surety, not for the King's jeopardy; and that they were also in safeguard, and there no longer should remain than till the matter were, not by the dukes only but also by all the other lords of the King's Council, indifferently examined and by other discretions ordered, and either judged or appeased. But one thing he advised them beware, that they judged not the matter too far forth before they knew the truth; nor, turning their private grudges into the common hurt, irritating and provoking men to anger and disturbing the King's coronation, towards which the Dukes were coming up, that they might peradventure bring the matter so far out of joint that it should never be brought in frame again. Which strife, if it should hap – as it were likely – to come to a field, though both parties were in all things equal, yet should the authority be on that side where the King is himself.

With these persuasions of the Lord Hastings, whereof part himself believed, of part he wist the contrary, these commotions were somewhat appeased. But specially by that the Dukes of Gloucester and Buckingham were so near, and came so shortly on with the King in no other manner, with no other voice or semblance, than to his coronation; causing the fame to be blown about that these lords and knights which were taken had contrived the destruction of the Dukes of Gloucester and Buckingham, and of other the noble blood of the realm, to the end that themselves would alone demean and govern the King at their pleasure. And for the colourable proof thereof, such of the Duke's servants as rode with the carts of their stuff that were taken (among which stuff no marvel, though some were harness, which at the breaking up of that household must needs either be brought away or cast away) they showed to the people all the way as they went: 'Lo, here be the barrels of harness that these traitors had privily conveyed in their carriage to destroy the noble lords withal.' This device – albeit that it made the matter to wise men more unlikely, well perceiving that the intenders of such a purpose would rather have had their harness on their back than to have bound them up in barrel – yet much part of the common people were therewith very well satisfied, and said it were almoise to hang them.

When the King approached near to the city, Edmund Shaa[33], goldsmith then Mayor, with William White and John Mathew, sheriffs, and all the other aldermen in scarlet, with five hundred horse of the citizens in violet, received him reverently at Hornsey; and riding from thence, accompanied him into the city, which he entered the fourth day of May, the first and last year of his reign. But the Duke of Gloucester bore him in open sight so reverently to the Prince, with all semblance of lowliness, that from the great obloquy in which he was so late before, he was suddenly fallen in so great trust that at the council next assembled he was made the only man chosen, and thought most meet, to be Protector of the King and his realm; so that were it destiny or were it folly, the lamb was betaken to the wolf to keep. At which council also the Archbishop of York, Chancellor of England, which had delivered up the great seal to the Queen, was thereof greatly reproved, and the seal taken from him and delivered to Dr Russell[34], Bishop of Lincoln, a wise man and a good, and of much experience, and one of the best learned men undoubtedly that England had in his time. Divers lords and knights were appointed to divers rooms. The Lord Chamberlain and some other kept still their offices that they had before.

Now all were it so that the Protector so sore thirsted for the finishing of that he had begun, that thought every day a year till it were achieved; yet dared he no further attempt as long as had but half his prey in his hand, well witting that if he deposed the one brother, all the Realm would fall to the other, if he either remained in sanctuary, or should haply be shortly conveyed to his further liberty. Wherefore incontinent at the next meeting of the lords at the council, he proposed to them that it was a heinous deed of the Queen, and proceeding of great malice towards the King's counsellors, that she should keep in sanctuary the King's brother from him whose special pleasure and comfort were to have his brother with him. And that by her done to no other intent, but to bring all the lords in obloquy and murmur of the people, as though they were not to be trusted with the King's brother, that by the assent of the nobles of the land were appointed as the King's nearest friends, to the tuition of his own royal person.

'The prosperity whereof stands,' quod he, 'not all in keeping from enemies or ill viand, but partly also in recreation and moderate pleasure, which he cannot in this tender youth take in the company of ancient persons, but in the familiar conversation of those that be neither far under nor far above his age, and nevertheless of estate convenient to accompany his noble majesty. Wherefore with whom rather than with his own brother? And if any man think this consideration light (which I think no man thinks that loves the King) let him consider that sometimes, without small things, greater cannot stand. And verily it redounds greatly to the dishonour both of the King's Highness and of all us that been about His Grace, to have it run in every man's mouth, not in this realm only but also in other lands (as evil words walk far) that the King's brother should be fain to keep sanctuary. For every man will ween that no man will so do for nought. And such evil opinion once fastened in men's hearts, hard it is to wrest out, and may grow to more grief than any man here can divine.

'Wherefore methink it were not worst to send to the Queen for the redress of this matter some honourable trusty man, such as both tenders the King's weal and the honour of his counsel, and is also in favour and credence with her. For all which considerations, none seems me more meetly than our reverent father here present, my Lord Cardinal[35], who may in this matter do most good of any man, if it please him to take the pain. Which I doubt not of his goodness he will not refuse, for the King's sake and ours, and wealth of the young Duke himself, the King's most honourable brother, and after my sovereign Lord himself, my most dear nephew; considered that thereby shall be ceased the slanderous rumour and obloquy now going and the hurts avoided that thereof might ensue, and much rest and quiet grow to all the realm. And if she be percase so obstinate and so precisely set upon her own will that neither his wise and faithful advertisement can move her, nor any man's reason content her – then shall we by mine advice, by the King's authority, fetch him out of that prison and bring him to his noble presence, in whose continual company he shall be so well cherished and so honourably entreated that all the world shall, to our honour and her reproach, perceive that it was only malice, frowardness or folly that caused her to keep him there. This is my mind in this matter for this time, except any of Your Lordships anything perceive to the contrary. For never shall I, by God's grace, so wed myself to mine own will, but that I shall be ready to change it upon your better advices.'

When the Protector had said, all the council affirmed that the motion was good and reasonable – and to the King and the Duke his brother, honourable – and a thing that should cease great murmur in the realm, if the mother might be by good means induced to deliver him. Which thing the Archbishop of York[36], whom they all agreed also to be thereto most convenient, took upon him to move her, and therein to do his uttermost devoir.

Howbeit if she could be in no wise entreated with her goodwill to deliver him, then thought he and such other as were of the spirituality present that it were not in any wise to be attempted to take him out against her will. For it would be a thing that should turn to the great grudge of all men – and high displeasure of God – if the privilege of that holy place should now be broken which had so many years been kept, which both kings and popes so good had granted, so many had confirmed; and which holy ground was, more than five hundred years ago by St Peter – his own person in spirit – accompanied with great multitude of angels, by night so specially hallowed and dedicate to God (for the proof whereof they have yet in the abbey St Peter's cope to show) that from that time hitherward was there never so undevout a king that dared that sacred place violate, or so holy a bishop that dared it presume to consecrate.

'And therefore,' quod the Archbishop of York[37], 'God forbid that any man should for anything earthly enterprise to break the immunity and liberty of that sacred sanctuary, that has been the safeguard of so many a good man's life. And I trust,' quod he, 'with God's grace, we shall not need it. But for any manner need, I would not we should do it. I trust that she shall be with reason contented, and all thing in good manner obtained. And if it happen that I bring it not so to pass, yet shall I toward it so far forth do my best that you shall all well perceive that no lack of my devoir, but the mother's dread and womanish fear, shall be the let.'

'Womanish fear, nay, womanish frowardness,' quod the Duke of Buckingham. 'For I dare take it upon my soul, she well knows she needs no such thing to fear, either for her son or for herself. For as for her, here is no man that will be at war with women. Would God some of the men of her kin were women too, and then should all be soon in rest. Howbeit, there is none of her kin the less loved for that they be her kin, but for their own evil deserving. And nevertheless, if we loved neither her nor her kin, yet were there no cause to think that we should hate the King's noble brother, to whose grace we ourselves be of kin; whose honour – if she as much desired as our dishonour, and as much regard took to his weal as to her own will – she would be as loath to suffer him from the King, as any of us be. For if she have any wit (as would God she had as goodwill as she has shrewd wit) she reckons herself no wiser than she thinks some that be here, of whose faithful mind she nothing doubts, but verily believes and knows that they would be as sorry of his harm as herself, and yet would have him from her if she bide there. And we all, I think, content that both be with her, if she come thence and bide in such place where they may with their honour be.

'Now then, if she refuse in the deliverance of him, to follow the counsel of them whose wisdom she knows, whose truth she well trusts, it is easy to perceive that frowardness lets her, and not fear. But go to, suppose that she fear (as who may let her to fear her own shadow), the more she fears to deliver him, the more ought we fear to leave him in her hands. For if she cast such fond doubts that she fear his hurt, then will she fear that he shall be fetched thence. For she will soon think that if men were set (which God forbid) upon so great a mischief, the sanctuary would little let them. Which good men might, as methinks, without sin somewhat less regard than they do.

'Now then, if she doubt lest he might be fetched from her,

is it not likely enough that she shall send him somewhere out of the realm? Verily, I look for none other. And I doubt not but she now as sore minds it, as we the let thereof. And if she might happen to bring that to pass, (as it were no great maistry, we letting her alone), all the world would say that we were a wise sort of counsellors about a king, that let his brother be cast away under our noses. And therefore I ensure you faithfully, for my mind I will rather – maugry her mind – fetch him away than leave him there till her frowardness or fond fear convey him away. And yet will I break no sanctuary therefore. For verily, since the privileges of that place and others like have been of long continued, I am not he that would be about to break them. And in good faith if they were now to begin, I would not be he that should be about to make them. Yet will I not say nay, but that it is a deed of pity that such men as the sea (or their evil debtors) have brought in poverty should have some place of liberty, to keep their bodies out of the danger of their cruel creditors. And also if the Crown happen (as it has done) to come in question, while either part takes others as traitors, I will well there be some places of refuge for both. But as for thieves, of which these places be full, and which never fall from the craft after they once fall thereto, it is pity the sanctuary should serve them – and much more mannequellers whom God bade to take from the altar and kill them, if their murder were wilful[38]. And where it is otherwise, there need we not the sanctuaries that God appointed in the old law. For if either necessity, his own defence, or misfortune draw him to that deed, a pardon serves which either the law grants of course, or the King of pity may.

'Then look me now how few sanctuary men there be whom any favourable necessity compelled to go thither. And then see on the other side what a sort there be commonly therein, of them whom wilful unthriftiness has brought to nought. What a rabble of thieves, murderers and malicious, heinous traitors, and that in two places specially: the one at the elbow of the city, the other in the very bowels.[39] I dare well avow it: weigh the good that they do with the hurt that comes of them, and you shall find it much better to lack both than have both. And this I say, although they were not abused as they now be and so long have been, that I fear me ever they will be while men be afraid to set their hands to the amendment – as though God and St Peter were the patrons of ungracious living.

'Now unthrifts riot and run in debt upon the boldness of these places; yea, and rich men run thither with poor men's goods – there they build, there they spend, and bid their creditors go whistle them. Men's wives run thither with their husbands' plate, and say they dare not abide with their husbands for beating. Thieves bring thither their stolen goods, and there live thereon; there devise they new robberies, nightly they steal out, they rob and reive and kill, and come in again as though those places gave them not only a safeguard for the harm they have done, but a licence also to do more. Howbeit, much of this mischief – if wise men would set their hands to it – might be amended, with great thank of God and no breach of the privilege. The residue – since so long ago I wot never what pope and what prince more piteous than politic has granted it, and other men since of a certain religious fear have not broken it – let us take a pain therewith, and let it a God's name stand in force, as far forth as reason will. Which is not fully so far forth as may serve to let us of the fetching forth of this noble man to his honour and wealth, out of that place in which he neither is nor can be a sanctuary man.

'A sanctuary serves always to defend the body of that man that stands in danger abroad, not of great hurt only, but also of lawful hurt. For against unlawful harms, never pope nor king intended to privilege any one place. For that privilege has every place. Know any man any place wherein it is lawful one man to do another wrong? That no man unlawfully take hurt, that liberty, the King, the law, and very nature forbids in every place, and makes to that regard for every man every place a sanctuary. But where a man is by lawful means in peril, there needs he the tuition of some special privilege, which is the only ground and cause of all sanctuaries. From which necessity this noble prince is far, whose love to his king nature and kindred proves, whose innocence to all the world his tender youth proves. And so sanctuary, as for him, neither none he needs nor also none can have. Men come not to sanctuary as they come to baptism, to require it by their godfathers. He must ask it himself that must have it. And reason, since no man has cause to have it but whose conscience of his own fault makes him feign need to require it, what will then have yonder babe? Which, even if he had discretion to require it if need were, I dare say would now be right angry with them that keep him there. And I would think without any scruple of conscience, without any breach of privilege, to be somewhat more homely with them that be there sanctuary men indeed. For if one go to sanctuary with another man's goods, why should not the King, leaving his body at liberty, satisfy the part of his goods even within the sanctuary? For neither king nor pope can give any place such a privilege that it shall discharge a man of his debts, being able to pay.'

And with that divers of the clergy that were present, whether they said it for his pleasure or as they thought, agreed plainly that by the law of God and of the church the goods of a sanctuary man should be delivered in payment of his debts, and stolen goods to the owner, and only liberty reserved him to get his living with the labour of his hands.

'Verily,' quod the Duke, 'I think you say very truth. And what if a man's wife will take sanctuary because she list to run from her husband? I would ween if she can allege no other cause, he may lawfully, without any displeasure to St Peter, take her out of St Peter's church by the arm. And if nobody may be taken out of sanctuary that says he will bide there, then if a child will take sanctuary because he fears to go to school, his master must let him alone. And as simple as that sample is, yet is there less reason in our case than in that. For therein, though it be a childish fear, yet is there at the leastwise some fear. And herein is there none at all. And verily I have often heard of sanctuary men. But I never heard erst of sanctuary children. And therefore as for the conclusion of my mind, who so may have deserved to need it, if they think it for their surety, let them keep it. But he can be no sanctuary man that neither has wisdom to desire it nor malice to deserve it, whose life or liberty can by no lawful process stand in jeopardy. And he that takes one out of sanctuary to do him good, I say plainly that he breaks no sanctuary.'

When the Duke had done, the temporal men whole – and good part of the spiritual also – thinking no hurt earthly meant towards the young babe, condescended in effect that if he were not delivered, he should be fetched. Howbeit, they thought it all best, in the avoiding of all manner of rumour, that the Lord Cardinal should first assay to get him with her goodwill. And thereupon all the council came to the Star Chamber at Westminster. And the Lord Cardinal, leaving the Protector with the council in the Star Chamber, departed into the sanctuary to the Queen, with divers other lords with him –

were it for the respect of his honour, or that she should by presence of so many perceive that this errand was not one man's mind; or were it for that the Protector intended not in this matter to trust any one man alone; or else that if she finally were determined to keep him, some of that company had haply secret instruction – incontinent, maugry her mind – to take him and to leave her no respite to convey him (which she was likely to mind after this matter broken to her, if her time would in any wise serve her).

When the Queen and these lords were come together in presence, the Lord Cardinal showed to her that it was thought – to the Protector and to the whole council – that her keeping of the King's brother in that place was the thing which highly sounded, not only to the great rumour of the people and their obloquy, but also to the importable grief and displeasure of the King's royal majesty. To whose grace it were as singular comfort to have his natural brother in company, as it was their both dishonour and all theirs and hers also to suffer him in sanctuary. As though the one brother stood in danger and peril of the other. And he showed her that the council therefore had sent him to her to require her the delivery of him, that he might be brought to the King's presence at his liberty, out of that place which they reckoned as a prison. And there should he be demeaned according to his estate. And she in this doing should both do great good to the realm, pleasure to the council, and profit to herself, succour to her friends[40] that were in distress, and over that (which he wist well she specially tendered), not only great comfort and honour to the King, but also to the young Duke himself, whose both great wealth it were to be together, as well for many greater causes as also for their both disport and recreation; which thing the Lord esteemed not slight, though it seem light, well pondering that their youth without recreation and play cannot endure; nor any stranger, for the convenience of their both ages and estates, so meetly in that point for any of them as either of them for other.

'My Lord,' quod the Queen, 'I say not nay, but that it were very convenient that this gentleman whom you require were in the company of the King, his brother. And in good faith methink it were as great commodity to them both, as for yet a while, to be in the custody of their mother, the tender age considered of the elder of them both, but specially the younger; which, besides his infancy that also needs good looking to, has a while been so sore diseased with sickness, and is so newly rather a little amended than well recovered, that I dare put no person earthly in trust with his keeping but myself only; considering that there is, as physicians say, and as we also find, double the peril in the recidivation that was in the first sickness, with which disease – nature being forelaboured, forewearied and weakened – waxes the less able to bear out a new surfeit. And albeit there might be found other that would haply do their best to him, yet is there none that either knows better how to order him than I that so long have kept him, or is more tenderly like to cherish him than his own mother that bore him.'

'No man denies, good madam,' quod the Cardinal, 'but that Your Grace were of all folk most necessary about your children, and so would all the council not only be content, but also glad that you were, if it might stand with your pleasure, to be in such place as might stand with their honour. But if you appoint yourself to tarry here, then think they yet more convenient, that the Duke of York were with the King honourably at his liberty to the comfort of them both, than here as a sanctuary man to their both dishonour and obloquy;

since there is not always so great necessity to have the child be with the mother, but that occasion may sometime be such that it should be more expedient to keep him elsewhere. Which in this well appears that at such time as your dearest son – then Prince and now King – should for his honour and good order of the country keep household in Wales, far out of your company, Your Grace was well content there with yourself.'

'Not very well content,' quod the Queen. 'And yet the case is not like, for the one was then in health, and the other is now sick. In which case I marvel greatly that my Lord Protector is so desirous to have him in his keeping, where if the child in his sickness miscarried by nature, yet might he run into slander and suspicion of fraud. And where they call it a thing so sore against my child's honour and theirs also that he bides in this place, it is all their honours there to suffer him bide where no man doubts he shall be best kept. And that is here, while I am here, which as yet intend not to come forth and jeopard myself after other of my friends; which would God were rather here in surety with me than I were there in jeopardy with them.'

'Why madam,' quod another lord, 'know you anything why they should be in jeopardy?'

'Nay, verily, sir,' quod she, 'nor why they should be in prison neither, as they now be. But it is I trow no great marvel though I fear, lest those that have not letted to put them in duress without colour, will let as little to procure their destruction without cause.'

The Cardinal made a countenance to the other lord that he should harp no more upon that string. And then said he to the Queen that he nothing doubted but that those lords of her honourable kin, which as yet remained under arrest, should upon the matter examined do well enough. And as toward her noble person, neither was nor could be any manner jeopardy.

'Whereby should I trust that?' quod the Queen. 'In that I am guiltless? As though they were guilty? In that I am with their enemies better beloved than they? When they hate them for my sake, in that I am so near of kin to the King? And how far be they off – if that would help, as God send grace it hurt not. And therefore as for me, I purpose not as yet to depart hence. And as for this gentleman my son, I mind that he shall be where I am till I see further. For I assure you, for that I see some men so greedy without any substantial cause to have him, this makes me much the more farder to deliver him.'

'Truly madam,' quod he, 'and the farder that you be to deliver him, the farder be other men to suffer you to keep him, lest your causeless fear might cause you further to convey him. And many be there that think that he can have no privilege in this place, which neither can have will to ask it nor malice to deserve it. And therefore they reckon no privilege broken, though they fetch him out. Which if you finally refuse to deliver him, I verily think they will – so much dread has My Lord, his uncle, for the tender love he bears him, lest Your Grace should hap to send him away.'

'Ah, sir,' quod the Queen, 'has the Protector so tender zeal to him that he fears nothing but lest he should escape him? Thinks he that I would send him hence, which neither is in the plight to send out; and in what place could I reckon him sure, if he be not sure in this, the sanctuary whereof was there never tyrant yet so devilish that dared presume to break? And I trust God, the most Holy St Peter, the guardian of this sanctuary, is as strong now to withstand his adversaries as ever he was. But my son can deserve no sanctuary, and therefore he cannot have it. Forsooth, he has found a goodly gloss by which that place that may defend a thief may not save an innocent. *But he is in no jeopardy nor has no need thereof.* Would God he had not. Trows the Protector – I pray God he may prove a Protector – trows he that I perceive not whereto his painted process draws? *It is not honourable that the Duke bide here; it were comfortable for them both that he were with his brother, because the King lacks a play-fellow* – be you sure. I pray God send them both better play-fellows than him that makes so high a matter upon such a trifling pretext; as though there could none be found to play with the King but if his brother – that has no lust to play for sickness – come out of sanctuary, out of his safeguard, to play with him; as though princes as young as they be could not play but with their peers, or children could not play but with their kindred, with whom for the more part they agree much worse than with strangers. *But the child cannot require the privilege* – who told him so? He shall hear him ask it, and he will. Howbeit this is a gay matter. Suppose he could not ask it, suppose he would not ask it, suppose he would ask to go out; if I say he shall not, if I ask the privilege but for myself, I say he that against my will takes out him, breaks the sanctuary. Serves this liberty for my person only, or for my goods too? You may not hence take my horse from me; and may you take my child from me? He is also my ward; for, as my learned counsel shows me, since he has nothing by descent held by knight's service, the law makes his mother his guardian. Then may no man, I suppose, take my ward from me out of sanctuary, without the breach of the sanctuary. And if my privilege could not serve him, nor he ask it for himself, yet since the law commits to me the custody of him, I may require it for him; except the law give a child a guardian only for his goods and his lands, discharging him of the care and safe keeping of his body, for which only both lands and goods serve.

'And if examples be sufficient to obtain privilege for my

child, I need not far to seek. For in this place in which we now be (and which is now in question whether my child may take benefit of it) mine other son, now King, was born, and kept in his cradle and preserved to a more prosperous fortune, which I pray God long to continue. And as all you know, this is not the first time that I have taken sanctuary[41]; for when My Lord, my husband, was banished and thrust out of his kingdom, I fled hither being great with child, and here I bore the Prince. And when My Lord my husband returned safe again and had the victory, then went I hence to welcome him home; and from hence I brought my babe the Prince to his father, when he first took him in his arms. And I pray God that my son's palace may be as great safeguard to him now reigning, as this place was sometime to the King's enemy. In which place I intend to keep his brother since man's law serves the guardian to keep the infant. The law of nature wills the mother keep her child. God's law privileges the sanctuary, and the sanctuary my son, since I fear to put him in the Protector's hands that has his brother already, and were – if both failed – inheritor to the Crown. The cause of my fear has no man to do to examine. And yet fear I no further than the law fears, which, as learned men tell me, forbids every man the custody of them by whose death he may inherit less land than a kingdom. I can no more, but whosoever he be that breaks this holy sanctuary, I pray God shortly send him need of sanctuary, when he may not come to it. For taken out of sanctuary would I not my mortal enemy were.'

The Lord Cardinal, perceiving that the Queen waxed ever the longer the further of, and also that she began to kindle and chafe, and speak sore biting words against the Protector, and such as he neither believed and was also loath to hear, he said to her for a final conclusion that he would no longer dispute the matter. But if she were content to deliver the Duke to him and to the other lords there present, he dared lay his own body and soul both in pledge, not only for his surety but also for his estate. And if she would give them a resolute answer to the contrary, he would forthwith depart therewithal, and shift whoso would with this business afterward; for he never intended more to move her in that matter, in which she thought that he, and all other save herself, lacked either wit or truth; wit, if they were so dull that they could nothing perceive what the Protector intended; truth, if they should procure her son to be delivered into his hands in whom they should perceive towards the child any evil intended.

The Queen with these words stood a good while in a great study. And forasmuch her seemed the Cardinal more ready to depart than some of the remnant, and the Protector himself ready at hand, so that she verily thought she could not keep him there, but that he should incontinent be taken thence; and to convey him elsewhere neither had she time to serve her, nor place determined, nor persons appointed, all thing unready – this message came on her so suddenly – nothing less looking for them to have him fetched out of sanctuary, which she thought to be now beset in such places about that he could not be conveyed out untaken; and partly as she thought it might fortune her fear to be false, so will she wast it was either needless or bootless; wherefore, if she should needs go from him, she deemed it best to deliver him. And over that, of the Cardinal's faith she nothing doubted, nor of some other lords neither, whom she there saw, which as she feared lest they might be deceived, so was she well assured they would not be corrupted. Then thought she it should yet make them the more warily to look to him, and the more circumspectly to see to his surety, if she with her own hands betook him to them of trust.

And at the last she took the young Duke by the hand, and said to the lords, 'My Lord,' quod she, 'and all My Lords, I neither am so unwise to mistrust your wits, nor so suspicious to mistrust your troths. Of which thing I purpose to make you such a proof as – if either of both lacked in you – might turn both me to great sorrow, the realm to much harm, and you to great reproach. For lo, here is,' quod she, 'this gentleman, whom I doubt not but I could here keep safe if I would, whatsoever any man say. And I doubt not also but there be some abroad – so deadly enemies to my blood – that if they wist where any of it lay in their own body, they would let it out. We have also had experience that the desire of a kingdom knows no kindred. The brother has been the brother's bane. And may the nephews be sure of their uncle? Each of these children is other's defence while they be asunder, and each of their lives lies in the other's body. Keep one safe and both be sure, and nothing for them both more perilous than to be both in one place. For what wise merchant adventures all his goods in one ship? All this notwithstanding, here I deliver him, and his brother in him, to keep into your hands, of whom I shall ask them both afore God and the world. Faithful you be, that wot I well, and I know well you be wise. Power and strength to keep him, if you list, neither lack you of yourself, nor can lack help in this cause. And if you cannot elsewhere, then may you leave him here. But only one thing I beseech you, for the trust that his father put in you ever, and for trust that I put in you now: that as far as you think that I fear too much, be you well aware that you fear not as far too little.'

And therewithal she said to the child, 'Farewell my own sweet son, God send you good keeping. Let me kiss you once yet before you go, for God knows when we shall kiss together again.' And therewith she kissed him, and blessed him, turned her back and wept and went her way, leaving the child weeping as fast.

When the Lord Cardinal and these other lords with him had received this young Duke, they brought him into the Star Chamber where the Protector took him in his arms and kissed him with these words: 'Now welcome, My Lord, even with all my very heart.' And he said in that of likelihood as he thought. Thereupon forthwith they brought him to the King, his brother, into the bishop's palace at Paul's, and from thence through the city honourably into the Tower, out of which after that day they never came abroad.

When the Protector had both the children in his hands, he opened himself more boldly, both to certain other men and also chiefly to the Duke of Buckingham, although I know that many thought that this Duke was privy to all the Protector's counsel even from the beginning. And some of the Protector's friends said that the Duke was the first mover of the Protector to this matter, sending a privy messenger to him straight after King Edward's death. But others again, which knew better the subtle wit of the Protector, deny that he ever opened his enterprise to the Duke until he had brought to pass the things before rehearsed. But when he had imprisoned the Queen's kinsfolk and got both her sons into his own hands, then he opened the rest of his purpose with less fear to them whom he thought meet for the matter, and specially to the Duke; who being won to his purpose, he thought his strength more than half increased.

The matter was broken to the Duke by subtle folks – and such as were their craft masters in the handling of such wicked devices – who declared to him that the young King was offended with him for his kinsfolk's sakes, and that if he were ever able, he would revenge them who would prick him forward thereunto, if they escaped (for they would remember their imprisonment). Or else if they were put to death, without doubt the young King would be careful for their deaths, whose imprisonment was grievous to him. And that with repenting the Duke should nothing avail, for there was no way left to redeem his offence by benefits, but he should sooner destroy himself than save the King, who with his brother and his kinsfolk he saw in such places imprisoned, as the Protector might with a beck destroy them all: and that it were no doubt but he would do it indeed, if there were any new enterprise attempted. And that it was likely that as the Protector had provided privy guard for himself, so had he spialles for the Duke and trains to catch him if he should be against him, and that, peradventure, from them whom he least suspected. For the state of things and the dispositions of men were then such that a man could not well tell whom he might trust or whom he might fear. These things and such like, being beaten into the Duke's mind, brought him to that point that where he had repented the way that he had entered, yet would he go forth in the same; since he had once begun, he would stoutly go through. And therefore to this wicked enterprise, which he believed could not be voided, he bent himself and went through; and determined that since the common mischief could not be amended, he would turn it as much as he might to his own commodity.

Then it was agreed that the Protector should have the Duke's aid to make him king, and that the Protector's only lawful son[42] should marry the Duke' daughter, and that the Protector should grant him the quiet possession of the Earldom of Hereford, which he claimed as his inheritance and could never obtain it in King Edward's time. Besides these requests of the Duke, the Protector of his own mind promised him a great quantity of the King's treasure and of his household stuff. And when they were thus at a point between themselves, they went about to prepare for the coronation of the young King ( as they would have it seem). And that they might turn both the eyes and minds of men from perceiving of their drifts otherwise, the lords, being sent for from all parts of the realm, came thick to that solemnity. But the Protector and the Duke, after that they had set the Lord Cardinal, the Archbishop of York (then Lord Chancellor), the Bishop of Ely, the Lord Stanley, and the Lord Hastings (then Lord Chamberlain) – with many other noblemen – to commune and devise about the coronation in one place; as fast were they in another place contriving the contrary, and to make the Protector king. To which council, albeit there were adhibit very few, and they very secret, yet began there here and there about some manner of muttering among the people, as though all should not long be well, though they neither wist what they feared nor wherefore; were it that before such great things, men's hearts of a secret instinct of nature misgive them – as the sea without wind swells of himself sometime before a tempest – or were it that some one man, haply somewhat perceiving, filled many men with suspicion, though he showed few men what he knew. Howbeit, somewhat the dealing itself made men to muse on the matter, though the council were close. For little and little all folk withdrew from the Tower, and drew to Crosby's place in Bishopsgate Street where the Protector kept his household. The Protector had the resort, the King in manner desolate. While some for their business made suit to them that had the doing, some were by their friends secretly warned that it might haply turn them to no good to be too much attendant about the King without the Protector's appointment; which removed also divers of the Prince's old servants from him, and set new about him.

Thus many things coming together – partly by chance, partly of purpose – caused at length not common people only, that wave with the wind, but wise men also, and some lords too, to mark the matter and muse thereon; so far forth that the Lord Stanley, that was after Earl of Derby, wisely mistrusted it and said to the Lord Hastings that he much misliked these two several councils.

'For while we,' quod he, 'talk of one matter in the one place, little wot we whereof they talk in the other place.'

'My Lord,' quod the Lord Hastings, 'on my life, never doubt you. For while one man is there which is never thence, never can there be thing once minded, that should sound amiss toward me, but it should be in mine ears before it were well out of their mouths.'

This meant he by Catesby[43], which was of his near secret counsel and whom he very familiarly used, and in his most weighty matters put no man in so special trust, reckoning himself to no man so lief; since he well wist there was no man to him so much beholden as was this Catesby, which was a man well learned in the laws of this land, and by the special favour of the Lord Chamberlain in good authority, and much rule bore in all the county of Leicester where the Lord Chamberlain's power chiefly lay. But surely great pity was it, that he had not had either more truth or less wit. For his dissimulation only, kept all that mischief up. In whom, if the Lord Hastings had not put so special trust, the Lord Stanley and he had departed with divers other lords and broken all the dance, for many ill signs that he saw, which he now construed all to the best, so surely thought he that there could be no harm towards him in that council intended where Catesby was.

And of truth the Protector and the Duke of Buckingham made very good semblance to the Lord Hastings, and kept him much in company. And undoubtedly the Protector loved him well and loath was to have lost him, saving for fear lest his life should have quailed their purpose. For which cause he moved Catesby to prove with some words cast out afar off, whether he could think it possible to win the Lord Hastings into their part. But Catesby, whether he assayed him or assayed him not, reported to them that he found him so fast and heard him speak so terrible words that he dared no further break. And of truth the Lord Chamberlain of very trust showed to Catesby the mistrust that other began to have in the matter. And therefore he, fearing lest their motions might with the Lord Hastings diminish his credence, whereunto only all the matter leant, procured the Protector hastily to rid him. And much the rather, for that he trusted by his death to obtain much of the rule that the Lord Hastings bore in his country; the only desire whereof was the allective that induced him to be partner and one special contriver of all this horrible treason.

Whereupon soon after – that is to wit, on the Friday the thirteenth day of June – many lords assembled in the Tower and there sat in council devising the honourable solemnity of the King's coronation; of which the time appointed so near approached that the pageants and subtleties were in making day and night at Westminster, and much victuals killed therefore that afterward was cast away. These lords so sitting together communing of this matter, the Protector came in among them, first about nine of the clock, saluting them courteously and excusing himself that he had been from them so long, saying merely that he had been asleep that day. And after a little talking with them, he said to the Bishop of Ely, 'My Lord, you have very good strawberries at your garden in Holborn, I require you let us have a mess of them.'

'Gladly, My Lord,' quod he; 'would God I had some better thing as ready to your pleasure as that.' And therewith in all the haste he sent his servant for a mess of strawberries. The Protector set the lords fast in communing, and thereupon, praying them to spare him for a little while, departed thence.

And soon, after one hour, between ten and eleven, he returned into the chamber among them all changed, with a wonderful sour, angry countenance – knitting the brows, frowning and frothing and gnawing on his lips – and so sat him down in his place; all the lords much dismayed and sore marvelling of this manner of sudden change, and what thing should him ail. Then when he had sat still a while, thus he began: 'What were they worthy to have that compass and imagine the destruction of me, being so near of blood to the King and Protector of his royal person and his realm?'

At this question, all the lords sat sore astonished, musing much by whom this question should be meant, of which every man wist himself clear. Then the Lord Chamberlain, as he that for the love between them thought he might be boldest with him, answered and said that they were worthy to be punished as heinous traitors, whatsoever they were. And all the other affirmed the same.

'That is,' quod he, 'yonder sorceress my brother's wife, and other with her;' meaning the Queen.

At these words many of the other lords were greatly abashed that favoured her. But the Lord Hastings was in his mind better content that it was moved by her than by any other whom he loved better, albeit his heart somewhat grudged that he was not afore made of counsel in this matter; as he was of the taking of her kindred and of their putting to death, which were by his assent before devised to be beheaded at Pomfret this selfsame day[44], in which he was not aware that it was by other devised that himself should the same day be beheaded at London.

Then said the Protector, 'You shall all see in what wise that sorceress and that other witch of her counsel, Shore's wife[45], with their affinity have by their sorcery and witchcraft wasted my body.' And therewith he plucked up his doublet sleeve to his elbow upon his left arm, where he showed a werish, withered arm – and small, as it was never other. And thereupon every man's mind sore misgave them, well perceiving that this matter was but a quarrel, for well they wist that the Queen was too wise to go about any such folly. And also, if she would, yet would she of all folk least make Shore's wife of counsel, whom of all women she most hated as that concubine whom the King, her husband, had most loved. And also no man was there present but well knew that his harm was ever such since his birth.

Nevertheless the Lord Chamberlain – which from the death of King Edward kept Shore's wife, on whom he somewhat doted in the King's life, saving as it is said he that while forbore her of reverence towards his King, or else of a certain kind of fidelity to his friend – answered and said, 'Certainly My Lord, if they have so heinously done, they be worthy heinous punishment.'

'What!' quod the Protector; 'you serve me I ween with "ifs" and with "ands". I tell you they have so done, and that I will make good on your body, traitor.'

And therewith, as in a great anger, he clapped his fist upon the board a great rap. At which token given, one cried

'Treason' without the chamber. Therewith a door clapped, and in come there rushing men in harness, as many as the chamber might hold. And anon the Protector said to the Lord Hastings, 'I arrest you, traitor.'

'What me, My Lord?' quod he.

'Yea, the traitor,' quod the Protector.

And another let fly at the Lord Stanley, which shrank at the stroke and fell under the table, or else his head had been cleft to the teeth; for as shortly as he shrank, yet ran the blood about his ears. Then were they all quickly bestowed in divers chambers except the Lord Chamberlain, whom the Protector bade speed and shrive him apace, 'For by St Paul,' quod he, 'I will not to dinner till I see your head off.' It booted him not to ask why, but heavily he took a priest at adventure and made a short shrift, for a longer would not be suffered; the Protector made so much haste to dinner, which he might not go to till this were done for the saving of his oath. So was he brought forth into the green beside the chapel within the Tower, and his head laid down upon a long log of timber and there stricken off; and afterward his body with the head entered at Windsor beside the body of King Edward, whose both souls our Lord pardon.

A marvellous case is it to hear either the warnings of that he should have voided, or the tokens of that he could not void. For the self night next before his death, the Lord Stanley sent a trusty secret messenger to him at midnight in all the haste, requiring him to rise and ride away with him, for he was disposed utterly no longer to bide; he had so fearful a dream in which him thought that a boar with his tusks so raced them both by the heads that the blood ran about both their shoulders. And forasmuch as the Protector gave the boar for his cognisaunce, this dream made so fearful an impression in his heart that he was thoroughly determined no longer to tarry, but had his horse ready, if the Lord Hastings would go with him to ride so far yet the same night that they should be out of danger before day.

'Aye, good lord,' quod the Lord Hastings to this messenger, 'leans My Lord your master so much to such trifles, and has such faith in dreams, which either his own fear fantasies or do rise in the night's rest by reason of his day thoughts? Tell him it is plain witchcraft to believe in such dreams; which, if they were tokens of things to come, why thinks he not that we might be as likely to make them true by our going, if we were caught and brought back (as friends fail fleers), for then had the boar a cause likely to race us with his tusks, as folk that fled for some falsehood; wherefore either is there no peril (nor none there is indeed) or if any be it is rather in going than biding. And if we should needs cost fall in peril one way or other, yet had I lever that men should see it were by other men's falsehood than think it were either our own fault or faint heart. And therefore go to your master, man, and commend me to him, and pray him be merry and have no fear; for I assure him I am as sure of the man that he wots of as I am of my own hand.'

'God send grace, sir,' quod the messenger, and went his way.

Certain is it also that in the riding towards the Tower the same morning in which he was beheaded, his horse twice or thrice stumbled with him almost to the falling; which thing, albeit each man wot well daily happens to them to whom no such mischance is toward, yet has it been of an old rite and custom observed as a token oftentimes, notably foregoing some great misfortune. Now this that follows was no warning, but an enemious scorn. The same morning before he were up, came a knight[46] to him, as it were of courtesy to accompany him to the council, but of truth sent by the Protector to haste him thitherward, with whom he was of secret confederacy in that purpose; a mean man at that time, and now of great authority. This knight, when it happed the Lord Chamberlain by the way to stay his horse and commune a while with a priest whom he met in the Tower Street, broke his tale and said merrily to him: 'What, My Lord, I pray you come on – whereto talk you so long with that priest? You have no need of a priest yet;' and therewith he laughed upon him, as though he would say, 'you shall have soon.' But so little wist the other what he meant, and so little mistrusted, that he was never merrier nor never so full of good hope in his life, which self thing is often seen a sign of change. But I shall rather let any thing pass me than the vain surety of man's mind so near his death.

Upon the very Tower wharf, so near the place where his head was off so soon after, there met he with one Hastings, a pursuivant of his own name. And of their meeting in that place, he was put in remembrance of another time in which it had happened them before to meet in like manner together in the same place. At which other time the Lord Chamberlain had been accused to King Edward by the Lord Rivers, the Queen's brother, in such wise that he was for the while (but it lasted not long) far fallen into the King's indignation, and stood in great fear of himself. And forasmuch as he now met this pursuivant in the same place – that jeopardy so well passed – it gave him great pleasure to talk with him thereof with whom he had before talked thereof, in the same place while he was therein.

And therefore he said, 'Ah, Hastings, are you remembered when I met you here once with a heavy heart?'

'Yea, My Lord,' quod he, 'that remember I well, and thanked be God they got no good, nor you no harm thereby.'

'You would say so,' quod he, 'if you knew as much as I know, which few know else as yet and more shall shortly.' That meant he by the lords of the Queen's kindred that were taken before, and should that day be beheaded at Pomfret; which he well wist, but nothing aware that the axe hung over his own head. 'In faith man,' quod he, 'I was never so sorry, nor never stood in so great dread in my life, as I did when you and I met here. And lo how the world is turned; now stand mine enemies in that danger (as you may hap to hear more hereafter) and I never in my life so merry, nor never in so great surety.'

O good God, the blindness of our mortal nature! When he most feared, he was in good surety; when he reckoned himself sure, he lost his life – and that within two hours after. Thus ended this honourable man: a good knight and a gentle, of great authority with his Prince, of living somewhat dissolute, plain and open to his enemy, and secret to his friend: easy to beguile, as he that of good heart and courage forestudied no perils; a loving man and passing well beloved; very faithful and trusty enough, trusting too much.

Now flew the fame of this lord's death swiftly through the city, and so forth further about like a wind in every man's ear. But the Protector, immediately after dinner, intending to set some colour upon the matter, sent in all the haste for many substantial men out of the city into the Tower. And at their coming, himself, with the Duke of Buckingham, stood harnessed in old ill-faring briginders, such as no man should ween that they would vouchsafe to have put upon their backs, except that some sudden necessity had constrained them. And then the Protector showed them that the Lord Chamberlain and other of his conspiracy had contrived to have suddenly destroyed him and the Duke there, the same day, in the council. And what they intended further was as yet not well known. Of which their treason he never had knowledge before ten of the clock the same forenoon. Which sudden fear drove them to put on for their defence such harness as came next to hand. And so had God helped them that the mischief turned upon them that would have done it. And this he required them to report.

Every man answered him fair, as though no man mistrusted the matter which of truth no man believed. Yet, for the further appeasing of the people's mind, he sent immediately after dinner in all the haste one herald of arms, with a proclamation to be made through the city in the King's name; containing that the Lord Hastings, with divers other of his traitorous purpose, had before conspired the same day to have slain the Lord Protector and the Duke of Buckingham sitting in the council, and after to have taken upon them to rule the King and the realm at their pleasure, and thereby to pill and spoil whom they list uncontrolled. And much matter was there in the proclamation devised to the slander of the Lord Chamberlain; as that he was an evil counsellor to the King's father, enticing him to many things highly redounding to the diminishing of his honour and to the universal hurt of his realm, by his evil company, sinister procuring, and ungracious example; as well in many other things as in the vicious living and inordinate abusion of his body both with many other and also specially with Shore's wife, which was one also of his most secret counsel of this heinous treason, with whom he lay nightly, and namely the night last passed next before his death; so that it was the less marvel if ungracious living brought him to an unhappy ending – which he was now put to, by the most dread commandment of the King's highness and of his honourable and faithful council, both for his demerits, being so openly taken in his falsely conceived treason, and also lest the delaying of his execution might have encouraged other mischievous persons, partners of his conspiracy, to gather and assemble themselves together in making some great commotion for his deliverance; whose hope now being by his well-deserved death politicly repressed, all the realm should by God's grace rest in good quiet and peace.

Now was this proclamation made within two hours after that he was beheaded, and it was so curiously indited and so fair written in parchment in so well a set hand, and therewith of itself so long a process, that every child might well perceive that it was prepared before. For all the time between his death and the proclaiming could scant have sufficed to the bare writing alone, all had it been but in paper and scribbled forth in haste at adventure. So that upon the proclaiming thereof, one that was schoolmaster of Paul's, of chance standing by and comparing the shortness of the time with the length of the matter, said to them that stood about him, 'Here is a gay goodly cast, foul cast away for haste.' And a merchant answered him that it was written by prophecy.

Now then by and by, as it were for anger not for courtesy, the Protector sent into the house of Shore's wife (for her husband dwelled not with her) and spoilt her of all that ever she had, above the value of two or three thousand marks, and sent her body to prison. And when he had a while laid to her for the manner sake that she went about to bewitch him, and that she was of counsel with the Lord Chamberlain to destroy him; in conclusion, when that no colour could fasten upon these matters, then he laid heinously to her charge the thing that she herself could not deny, that all the world wist was true, and that nevertheless every man laughed at to hear it then so suddenly so highly taken – that she was nought of her body.

And for this cause (as a goodly continent prince, clean and faultless of himself, sent out of heaven into this vicious world for the amendment of men's manners) he caused the Bishop of London to put her to open penance, going before the cross in procession upon a Sunday with a taper in her hand; in which she went in countenance and pace demure so womanly, and albeit she were out of all array save her kirtle only, yet went she so fair and lovely, namely while the wondering of the people cast a comely rud in her cheeks (of which she before had most miss) that her great shame won her much praise among those that were more amorous of her body than curious of her soul. And many good folk also, that hated her living and glad were to see sin corrected, yet pitied they more her penance than rejoiced therein, when they considered that the Protector procured it more of a corrupt intent than any virtuous affection.

This woman was born in London, worshipfully friended, honestly brought up, and very well married (saving somewhat too soon); her husband an honest citizen, young and goodly and of good substance. But forasmuch as they were coupled before she were well ripe, she not very fervently loved, for whom she never longed. Which was haply the thing that the more easily made her incline to the King's appetite when he required her. Howbeit, the respect of his royalty, the hope of gay apparel, ease, pleasure and other wanton wealth, was soon able to pierce a soft, tender heart. But when the King had abused her, anon her husband (as he was an honest man and one that could his good, not presuming to touch a king's concubine) left her up to him altogether. When the King died the Lord Chamberlain took her, which in the King's days, albeit he was sore enamoured upon her, yet he forbore her, either for reverence or for a certain friendly faithfulness.

Proper she was and fair; nothing in her body that you would have changed, but if you would have wished her somewhat higher. Thus say they that knew her in her youth, albeit some that now see her (for yet she lives) deem her never to have been well visaged. Whose judgement seems me somewhat like as though men should guess the beauty of one long before departed by her scalp, taken out of the charnel house; for now is she old, lean, withered and dried up, nothing left but rivelled skin and hard bone. And yet being even such, whoso well advise her visage might guess and devise which parts, how filled, would make it a fair face.

Yet she delighted not men so much in her beauty as in her pleasant behaviour. For a proper wit had she, and could both read well and write; merry in company, ready and quick of answer, neither mute nor full of babble, sometime taunting without displeasure, and not without disport. The King would say that he had three concubines, which in three diverse properties diversely excelled. One the merriest, another the wiliest, the third the holiest harlot in his realm, as one whom no man could get out of the church lightly to any place but it were to his bed. The other two were somewhat greater personages, and nevertheless of their humility content to be nameless and to forbear the praise of those properties. But the merriest was this Shore's wife, in whom the King therefore took special pleasure. For many he had, but her he loved, whose favour, to say truth (for sin it were to belie the devil) she never abused to any man's hurt, but to many a man's comfort and relief. Where the King took displeasure, she would mitigate and appease his mind; where men were out of favour, she would bring them in his grace; for many that had highly offended, she obtained pardon. Of great forfeitures she got men remission. And finally in many weighty suits she stood many men in great stead, either for no or very small rewards, and those rather gay than rich; either for that she was content with the deed self well done; or for that she delighted to be sued to, and to show what she was able to do with the King; or for that wanton women and wealthy be not always covetous.

I doubt not some shall think this woman too slight a thing to be written of and set among the remembrances of great matters; which they shall specially think that haply shall esteem her only by that they now see her. But me seems the chance so much the more worthy to be remembered, in how much she is now in the more beggarly condition – unfriended and worn out of acquaintance, after good substance, after as great favour with the Prince, after as great suit and seeking to with all those that those days had business to speed, as many other men were in their times, which be now famous only by the infamy of their ill deeds. Her doings were not much less, albeit they be much less remembered because they were not so evil. For men use, if they have an evil turn, to write it in marble; and whoso doth us a good turn, we write it in dust; which is not worst proved by her, for at this day she begs of many at this day living, that at this day had begged if she had not been.

Now was it so devised by the Protector and his council that the self day[47] in which the Lord Chamberlain was beheaded in the Tower of London, and about the selfsame hour, was there not without his assent beheaded at Pomfret the fore-remembered lords and knights that were taken from the King at Northampton and Stony Stratford. Which thing was done in the presence and by the order of Sir Richard Ratcliff, knight, whose service the Protector specially used in the council, and in the execution of such lawless enterprises, as a man that had been long secret with him; having experience of the world and a shrewd wit, short and rude in speech, rough and boisterous of behaviour, bold in mischief, as far from pity as from all fear of God. This knight, bringing them out of the prison to the scaffold, and showing to the people about that they were traitors – not suffering them to speak and declare their innocence lest their words might have inclined men to pity them and to hate the Protector and his part – caused them hastily without judgement, process, or manner of order to be beheaded, and without other earthly guilt but only that they were good men, too true to the King and too nigh to the Queen.

Now when the Lord Chamberlain and these other lords were thus beheaded and rid out of the way, then thought the Protector that – while men mused what the matter meant, while the lords of the realm were about him out of their own strengths, while no man wist what to think nor whom to trust, before ever they should have space to dispute and digest the matter and make parties – it were best hastily to pursue his purpose and put himself in possession of the Crown, before men could have time to devise any ways to resist. But now was all the study by what means this matter, being of itself so heinous, might be first broken to the people in such wise that it might be well taken. To this counsel they took diverse, such as they thought meetly to be trusted, likely to be induced to the part, and able to stand them in stead, either by power or policy.

Among whom they made of counsel Edmund Shaa, knight,

then Mayor of London, which upon trust of his own advancement, whereof he was of a proud heart highly desirous, should frame the city to their appetite. Of spiritual men they took such as had wit, and were in authority among the people for opinion of their learning, and had no scrupulous conscience. Among these had they John Shaa[48], clerk, brother to the Mayor, and Friar Penker[49], Provincial of the Augustine Friars; both doctors of divinity, both great preachers, both of more learning than virtue, of more fame than learning. For they were before greatly esteemed among the people, but after that never.

Of these two the one had a sermon in praise of the Protector before the coronation, the other after; both so full of tedious flattery that no man's ears could abide them. Penker in his sermon so lost his voice that he was fain to leave off and come down in the midst. Doctor Shaa by his sermon lost his honesty, and soon after his life, for very shame of the world into which he dared never after come abroad. But the friar forced for no shame, and so it harmed him the less. Howbeit, some doubt and many think that Penker was not of counsel of the matter before the coronation, but, after the common manner, fell to flattery after; namely since his sermon was not incontinent upon it, but at St Mary Hospital at the Easter after. But certain is it that Dr Shaa was of counsel in the beginning – so far forth that they determined that he should first break the matter in a sermon at Paul's Cross, in which he should by the authority of his preaching incline the people to the Protector's ghostly purpose.

But now was all the labour and study in the device of some convenient pretext for which the people should be content to depose the Prince and accept the Protector for king, in which divers things they devised. But the chief thing and the weighty of all that invention rested in this: that they should allege bastardy, either in King Edward himself, or in his children, or both, so that he should seem disabled to inherit the Crown by the Duke of York, and the Prince by him. To lay bastardy in King Edward sounded openly to the rebuke of the Protector's own mother[50], which was mother to them both, for in that point could be no other colour but to pretend that his own mother was one adulteress – which, not withstanding to further this purpose, he letted not. But nevertheless, he would the point should be less and more favourably handled – not even fully plain and directly, but that the matter should be touched a slope, craftily, as though men spared in that point to speak all the truth for fear of his displeasure. But the other point, concerning the bastardy that they devised to surmise in King Edward's children – that, would he, should be openly declared and enforced to the uttermost. The colour and pretext whereof cannot be well perceived but if we first repeat you some things long before done about King Edward's marriage[51].

After that King Edward the Fourth had deposed King Henry the Sixth and was in peaceable possession of the realm, determining himself to marry (as it was requisite both for himself and for the realm), he sent over in embassy the Earl of Warwick with other noblemen in his company to Spain, to entreat and conclude a marriage between King Edward and the King's daughter[52] of Spain. In which thing the Earl of Warwick found the parties so toward and willing that he speedily, according to his instructions, without any difficulty brought the matter to a very good conclusion.

Now happed it that in the mean season, there came, to make a suit by petition to the King, Dame Elizabeth Grey – which was after his Queen, at that time a widow – born of noble blood, specially by her mother which was Duchess of Bedford before she married the Lord Woodville her father. Howbeit, this Dame Elizabeth, herself being in service with Queen Margaret[53], wife to King Henry the Sixth, was married to one John Grey[54], a squire whom King Henry made knight upon the field that he had on Shrove Tuesday at St Albans against King Edward. And little while enjoyed he that knighthood, for he was at the same field slain. After which done, and the Earl of Warwick being in his embassy about the afore-remembered marriage, this poor Lady made humble suit to the King that she might be restored to such small lands as her late husband had given her in jointure.

Whom, when the King beheld and heard her speak – as she was both fair, of a good favour, moderate of stature, well made and very wise – he not only pitied her, but also waxed enamoured on her. And taking her afterward secretly aside, began to enter in talking more familiarly. Whose appetite, when she perceived, she virtuously denied him. But that did she so wisely and with so good manner, and words so well set, that she rather kindled his desire than quenched it. And finally after many a meeting, much wooing and many great promises, she well espied the King's affection towards her so greatly increased that she dared somewhat the more boldly say her mind, as to him whose heart she perceived more finely set than to fall off for a word. And in conclusion she showed him plain that as she wist herself too simple to be his wife, so thought she herself too good to be his concubine. The King, much marvelling of her constancy, as he that had not been wont elsewhere to be so stiffly said nay, so much esteemed her continence and chastity that he set her virtue in the stead of possession and riches. And thus taking counsel of his desire, determined in all possible haste to marry her. And after he was thus appointed and had between them twain ensured her, then asked he counsel of his other friends – and that in such manner as they might easy perceive it booted not greatly to say nay.

Notwithstanding, the Duchess of York, his mother, was so sore moved therewith that she dissuaded the marriage as much as she possibly might, alleging that it was in his honour, profit and surety also to marry in a noble progeny out of his realm, whereupon depended great strength to his estate by the affinity and great possibility of increase of his possessions; and that he could not well otherwise do, standing that the Earl of Warwick had so far moved already – which were not likely to take it well, if all his voyage were in such wise frustrated and his appointments deluded.

And she said also that it was not princely to marry his own subject, no great occasion leading thereunto, no possessions or other commodities depending thereupon, but only as it were a rich man that would marry his maid only for a little wanton dotage upon her person. In which marriage many more commend the maiden's fortune than the master's wisdom. And yet therein she said was more honesty than honour in this marriage, forasmuch as there is between no merchant and his own maid so great difference as between the King and this widow; in whose person albeit there was nothing to be misliked, yet was there she said 'nothing so excellent but it might be found in divers other that were more meetly,' quod she, 'for your estate, and maidens also; whereas the only widowhood of Elizabeth Grey, though she were in all other thing convenient for you, should yet suffice, as me seems, to refrain you from her marriage, since it is an unsitting thing – and a very blemish and high disparagement to the sacred majesty of a prince that ought as nigh to approach priesthood in cleanness as he does in dignity – to be defouled with bigamy in his first marriage.'

The King, when his mother had said, made her answer – part in earnest, part in play merrily – as he that wist himself out of her rule; and albeit he would gladly that she should take it well, yet was at a point in his own mind, took she it well or otherwise. Howbeit, somewhat to satisfy her he said that albeit marriage, being a spiritual thing, ought rather to be made for the respect of God, where his grace inclines the parties to love together (as he trusted it was in his) than for the regard of any temporal advantage; yet nevertheless him seemed that this marriage, even worldly considered, was not unprofitable. For he reckoned the amity of no earthly nation so necessary for him as the friendship of his own, which he thought likely to bear him so much the more hearty favour in that he disdained not to marry with one of his own land. And yet if outward alliance were thought so requisite, he would find the means to enter thereinto much better by other of his kin, where all the parties could be contented, than to marry himself whom he should haply never love, and for the possibility of more possessions lose the fruit and pleasure of this that he had already.

'For small pleasure takes a man of all that ever he has beside, if he be wived against his appetite. And I doubt not,' quod he, 'but there be as you say other that be in every point comparable with her. And therefore I let not them that like them to wed them. No more is it reason that it mislike any man that I marry where it likes me. And I am sure that my cousin of Warwick neither loves me so little to grudge at that I love, nor is so unreasonable to look that I should, in choice of a wife, rather be ruled by his eye than by mine own, as though I were a ward that were bound to marry by the appointment of a guardian. I would not be a king with that condition, to forbear mine own liberty in choice of my own marriage. As for possibility of more inheritance by new affinity in strange lands, it is often the occasion of more trouble than profit. And we have already title by that means to so much as suffices to get and keep well in one man's days. That she is a widow and has already children, by God's blessed Lady, I am a bachelor and have some too;[55] and so each of us has a proof that neither of us is like to be barren. And therefore, madam, I pray you be content. I trust in God she shall bring forth a young prince that shall please you. And as for the bigamy, let the bishop hardly lay it in my way when I come to take orders. For I understand it is forbidden a priest, but I never wist it yet that it was forbidden a prince.

The Duchess with these words nothing appeased, and seeing the King so set thereon that she could not pull him back, so highly she disdained it that under pretext of her duty to Godward she devised to disturb this marriage, and rather to help that he should marry one Dame Elizabeth Lucy, whom the King had also not long before gotten with child. Wherefore the King's mother objected openly against his marriage, as it were in discharge of her conscience, that the King was sure to Dame Elizabeth Lucy, and her husband before God. By reason of which words, such obstacle was made in the matter that either the bishops dared not, or the King would not, proceed to the solemnisation of this wedding till these same were clearly purged, and the truth well and openly testified. Whereupon Dame Elizabeth Lucy was sent for. And albeit that she was by the King's mother and many other put in good comfort to affirm that she was ensured to the King, yet when she was solemnly sworn to say the truth she confessed that they were never ensured. Howbeit, she said His Grace spoke so loving words to her that she verily hoped he would have married her. And that if it had not been for such kind words, she would never have shown such kindness to him to let him so kindly get her with child. This examination solemnly taken, when it was clearly perceived that there was no impediment, the King, with great feast and honourable solemnity, married Dame Elizabeth Grey, and her crowned Queen that was his enemy's wife, and many time had prayed full heartily for his loss. In which God loved her better than to grant her her boon.

But when the Earl of Warwick understood of this marriage, he took it so highly that his embassy was deluded that, for very anger and disdain, he at his return assembled a great puissaunce against the King, and came so fast upon him before he could be able to resist, that he was fain to void the realm and flee into Holland for succour; where he remained for the space of two years,[56] leaving his new wife in Westminster in sanctuary, where she was delivered of Edward the Prince, of whom we before have spoken. In which meantime the Earl of Warwick took out of prison and set up again Henry the Sixth, which was before by King Edward deposed – and that much what by the power of the Earl of Warwick, which was a wise man and a courageous warrior, and of such strength (what for his lands, his alliance, and favour with all the people) that he made kings and put down kings almost at his pleasure, and not impossible to have attained it himself if he had not reckoned it a greater thing to make a king than to be a king. But nothing lasts always: for in conclusion King Edward returned and – with much less number than he had – at Barnet on the Easter Day field[57] slew the Earl of Warwick with many other great estates of that party, and so stably attained the Crown again that he peaceably enjoyed it until his dying day; and in such plight left it that it could not be lost but by the discord of his very friends, or falsehood of his feigned friends.

I have rehearsed this business about this marriage somewhat the more at length because it might thereby the better appear how slipper a ground the Protector built his colour, by which he pretended King Edward's children to be bastards. But that invention, simple as it was, it liked them to whom it sufficed to have somewhat to say, while they were sure to be compelled to no larger proof than themselves list to make.

Now then, as I began to show you, it was by the Protector and his council concluded that this Dr Shaa should, in a sermon at Paul's Cross, signify to the people that neither King Edward himself nor the Duke of Clarence were lawfully begotten, nor were not the very children of the Duke of York, but gotten unlawfully by other persons by the adultery of the Duchess, their mother; and that also Dame Elizabeth Lucy was verily the wife of King Edward, and so the Prince and all his children bastards that were gotten upon the Queen.

According to this device, Dr Shaa, the Sunday after at Paul's Cross, in a great audience (as always assembled great number to his preaching) he took for his theme *Spuria vitulamina non agent radices altas;* that is to say, 'bastard slips shall never take deep root'. Thereupon, when he had shown the great grace that God gives and secretly infounds in the right generation after the laws of matrimony, then declared he that commonly those children lacked that grace – and for the punishment of their parents were for the most part unhappy – which were gotten in baste and specially in adultery. Of which, though some by the ignorance of the world and the truth hid from knowledge inherited for the season other men's lands, yet God always so provides that it continues not in their blood long but – the truth coming to light – the rightful inheritors be restored and the bastard slip pulled up before it can be rooted deep. And when he had laid for the proof and confirmation of this sentence certain examples taken out of the Old Testament and other ancient histories, then began he to descend into the praise of the Lord Richard, late Duke of York, calling him father to the Lord Protector, and declared the title of his heirs to the Crown, to whom it was after the death of King Henry the Sixth entailed by authority of Parliament. Then showed he that his very right heir of his body, lawfully begotten, was only the Lord Protector. For he declared then that King Edward was never lawfully married to the Queen, but was, before God, husband to Dame Elizabeth Lucy, and so his children bastards. And besides that, neither King Edward himself nor the Duke of Clarence, among those that were secret in the household, were reckoned very surely for the children of the noble Duke, as those that by their favours more resembled other known men than him, from whose virtuous conditions he said also that King Edward was far off. But the Lord Protector, he said, that very noble prince, the special pattern of knightly prowess, as well in all princely behaviour as in the lineaments and favour of his visage, represents the very face of the noble Duke his father. 'This is,' quod he, 'the father's own figure; this is his own countenance, the very print of his visage, the sure undoubted image, the plain express likeness of that noble Duke.'

Now was it before devised that in the speaking of these words, the Protector should have come in among the people to the sermonward, to the end that those words, meeting with his presence, might have been taken among the hearers as though the Holy Ghost had put them in the preacher's mouth, and should have moved the people even there to cry 'King Richard! King Richard!' – that it might have been after said that he was specially chosen by God and in manner by miracle. But this device quailed, either by the Protector's negligence or the preacher's overmuch diligence. For while the Protector found by the way tarrying, lest he should prevent those words, and the Doctor, fearing that he should come before his sermon could come to those words, hasted his matter thereto; he was come to them and past them and entered into other matters before the Protector came. Whom when he beheld coming, he suddenly left the matter with which he was in hand and without any deduction thereunto, out of all order and out of all frame, began to repeat those words again: 'This is the very noble prince, the special patron of knightly prowess, which as well in all princely behaviour as in the lineaments and favour of his visage, represents the very face of the noble Duke of York, his father. This is the father's own figure, this his own countenance, the very print of his visage, the sure undoubted image, the plain express likeness of the noble Duke, whose remembrance can never die while he lives.'

While these words were in speaking, the Protector, accompanied with the Duke of Buckingham, went through the people into the place where the doctors commonly stand in the upper storey, where he stood to hearken the sermon. But the people were so far from crying 'King Richard!' that they stood as they had been turned into stone, for wonder of this shameful sermon. After which once ended, the preacher got him home and never after dared look out for shame, but kept him out of sight like an owl. And when he once asked one that had been his old friend, what the people talked of him – all were it that his own conscience well showed him that they talked no good – yet when the other answered him that there was in every man's mouth spoken of him much shame, it so struck him to the heart that within few days after he withered and consumed away.

Then on the Tuesday following this sermon, there came to the Guildhall in London the Duke of Buckingham, accompanied with divers lords and knights, more than haply knew the message that they brought. And there in the east end of the hall, where the Mayor keeps the hustings[58], the Mayor and all the aldermen being assembled about him, all the commons of the city gathered before them, after silence commanded upon great pain in the Protector's name, the Duke stood up and (as he was neither unlearned and of nature marvellously well spoken) he said to the people with a clear and a loud voice in this manner of wise:

'Friends, for the zeal and hearty favour that we bear you, we become to break to you of a matter right great and weighty, and no less weighty than pleasing to God, and profitable to all the realm; nor to no part of the realm more profitable than to you, the citizens of this noble city. For why? That thing that we wot well you have long time lacked and sore longed for, that you would have given great good for, that you would have gone far to fetch – that thing we be come hither to bring you, without your labour, pain, cost, adventure or jeopardy. What thing is that? Certes, the surety of your own bodies, the quiet of your wives and your daughters, the safeguard of your goods – of all which things in times passed you stood ever more in doubt. For who was there of you all that would reckon himself lord of his own good, among so many grennes and traps as was set therefore, among so much pilling and polling, among so many taxes and tallages, of which there was never end, and oftentime no need; or if any were, it rather grew of riot and unreasonable waste than any necessary or honourable charge. So that there was daily pilled, from good men and honest, great substance of goods to be lashed out among unthrifts so far forth that fifteenths sufficed not, nor any usual names of known taxes; but under an easy name of benevolence and goodwill, the commissioners so much of every man took as no man would with his goodwill have given – as though the name of benevolence had signified that every man should pay, not what himself of his goodwill list to grant, but what the King of his goodwill list to take; which never asked little, but every thing was hawsed above the measure; amercements turned into fines, fines into ransoms, small trespass to misprision, misprision into treason.

'Whereof, I think, no man looks that we should remember you of examples by name, as though Burdet[59] were forgotten, that was – for a word spoken in haste – cruelly beheaded, by the misconstruing of the laws of this realm for the Prince's pleasure; with no less honour to Markham[60], then Chief Justice, that left his office rather than he would assent to that judgement, than to the dishonesty of those that either for fear or flattery gave that judgement. What of Cook[61], your own worshipful neighbour, alderman and Mayor of this noble city? Who is of you either so negligent that he knows not, or so forgetful that he remembers not, or so hard-hearted that he pities not, that worshipful man's loss? What speak we of loss? His utter spoil and underserved destruction, only for that it happed those to favour him whom the Prince favoured not. We need not I suppose to rehearse of these any more by name, since there be, I doubt not, many here present that either in themselves or their nigh friends have known as well their goods as their persons greatly endangered, either by feigned quarrels or small matters aggrieved with heinous names.

'And also there was no crime so great of which there could lack a pretext. For since the King, preventing the time of his inheritance, attained the Crown by battle, it sufficed in a rich man – for a pretext of treason – to have been of kindred or alliance, near familiarity or leger acquaintance with any of those that were at any time the King's enemies; which was at one time and other more than half the realm. Thus were neither your goods in surety and yet they brought your bodies in jeopardy, beside the common adventure of open war, which albeit that it is ever the will and occasion of much mischief, yet is it never so mischievous as where any people fall at distance among themselves, nor in no earthly nation so deadly and so pestilent as when it happens among us; and among us never so long continued dissension, nor so many battles in the season, nor so cruel and deadly fought, as was in the King's days that dead is, God forgive it his soul. In whose time and by whose occasion, what about the getting of the garland, keeping it, losing and winning again, it has cost more English blood than has twice the winning of France. In which inward war among ourselves has been so great effusion of the ancient noble blood of this realm that scarcely the half remains, to the great enfeebling of this noble land; beside many a good town ransacked and spoilt by them that have been going to the field or coming from thence. And peace long after not much surer than war. So that no time was there in which rich men for their money and great men for their lands, or some other for some fear or some displeasure, were not out of peril. For whom trusted he that mistrusted his own brother? Whom spared he that killed his own brother?[62] Or who could perfectly love him, if his own brother could not?

'What manner of folk he most favoured, we shall for his honour spare to speak of; howbeit, this wot you well all, that whoso was best, bore always least rule, and more suit was in his days to Shore's wife, a vile and abominable strumpet, than to all the lords in England, except to those that made her their proctor; which simple woman was well named and honest till the King, for his wanton lust and sinful affection, bereft her from her husband, a right honest substantial young man among you. And in that point – which in good faith I am sorry to speak of, saving that it is in vain to keep in counsel that thing that all men know – the King's greedy appetite was insatiable, and everywhere over all the realm intolerable. For no woman was there anywhere, young or old, rich or poor, whom he set his eye upon – in whom he anything liked, either person or favour, speech, pace or countenance – but without any fear of God or respect of his honour, murmur or grudge of the world, he would importunely pursue his appetite and have her, to the great destruction of many a good woman and great dolour to their husband and their other friends; which, being honest people of themselves, so much regard the cleanness of their house, the chastity of their wives and their children, that them were lever to lose all that they have beside than to have such a villainy done them.

'And all were it that with this and other importable dealing, the realm was in every part annoyed; yet specially you here, the citizens of this noble city, as well for that among you is most plenty of all such things as minister matter to such injuries, as for that you were nearest at hand, since that near here about was commonly his most abiding. And yet be you the people whom he had as singular cause well and kindly to entreat as any part of his realm, not only for that the Prince, by this noble city – as his special chamber and the special well-renowned city of his realm – much honourable fame receives among all other nations; but also for that you, not without your great cost and sundry perils and jeopardies in all his wars, bore ever your special favour to his part, which – your kind minds borne to the House of York, since he has nothing worthily acquitted – there is of that House that now[63] by God's grace better shall; which thing to show you is the whole sum and effect of this our present errand.

'It shall not, I wot well, need that I rehearse you again that you have already heard, of him that can better tell it, and of whom I am sure you will better believe it. And reason is that it so be. I am not so proud to look therefore that you should reckon my words of as great authority as the preachers of the word of God; namely a man so cunning and so wise that no man better wot what he should say, and thereto so good and virtuous that he would not say the thing which he wist he should not say in the pulpit, namely, into which no honest man comes to lie. Which honourable preacher you well remember substantially declared to you at Paul's Cross on Sunday last passed, the right and title that the most excellent Prince Richard, Duke of Gloucester, now Protector of this realm, has to the Crown and kingdom of the same. For as that worshipful man groundly made open to you, the children of King Edward the Fourth were never lawfully begotten, forasmuch as the King (living his very wife, Dame Elizabeth Lucy) was never lawfully married to the Queen their mother, whose blood, saving that he set voluptuous pleasure before his honour, was full unmeetly to be matched with his; and the mingling of whose bloods together has been the effusion of great part of the noble blood of this realm. Whereby it may well seem that marriage not well made, of which there is so much mischief grown. For lack of which lawful coupling and also of other things which the said worshipful Doctor rather signified than fully explained, and which things shall not be spoken for me (as the thing wherein every man forbears to say that he knows, in avoiding displeasure of my noble Lord Protector, bearing as nature requires a filial reverence to the Duchess his mother); for these causes, I say, before remembered, that is to wit – for lack of other issue lawfully coming of the late noble Prince – Richard, Duke of York, to whose royal blood the Crown of England and of France is by the high authority of Parliament entailed, the right and title of the same is, by the just course of inheritance according to the common law of this land, devolute and come to the most excellent Prince the Lord Protector, as to the very lawfully begotten son of the fore-remembered noble Duke of York.

'Which thing well considered, and the great knightly prowess pondered, with manifold virtues which in his noble person singularly abound, the nobles and commons also of this realm – and specially of the north parts – not willing any bastard blood to have the rule of the land nor the abusions before in the same used any longer to continue, have condescended and fully determined to make humble petition to the most puissant prince, the Lord Protector, that it may like His Grace at our humble request to take upon him the guiding and governance of this realm, to the wealth and increase of the same, according to his very right and just title. Which thing I wot it well he will be loath to take upon him, as he whose wisdom well perceives the labour and study both of mind and of body that shall come therewith to whomsoever so well occupy that room, as I dare say he will if he take it. Which room, I warn you well, is no child's office; and that the great wise man[64] well perceived when he said, *Veh regno cuius rex puer est;* "Woe is that realm that has a child to their king."

'Wherefore so much the more cause have we to thank God that this noble personage, which is so righteously entitled thereunto, is of so sad age, and thereto of so great wisdom joined with so great experience; which albeit he will be loath, as I have said, to take it upon him, yet shall he to our petition in that behalf the more graciously incline if you, the worshipful citizens of this the chief city of this realm, join with us, the nobles, in our said request. Which for your own weal we doubt not but you will; and nevertheless I heartily pray you so to do, whereby you shall do great profit to all this realm beside in choosing them so good a king, and to yourselves special commodity, to whom His Majesty shall ever after bear so much the more tender favour, in how much he shall perceive you the more prone and benevolently minded towards his election. Wherein, dear friends, what mind you have, we require you plainly to show us.'

When the Duke had said, and looked that the people, whom he hoped that the Mayor had framed before, should after this proposition made have cried 'King Richard! King Richard!' – all was hushed and mute, and not one word answered thereunto. Wherewith the Duke was marvellously abashed, and taking the Mayor near to him, with the other that were about him privy to that matter, said to them softly, 'What means this, that this people be so still?'

'Sir,' quod the Mayor, 'percase they perceive you not well.'

'That shall we mend,' quod he, 'if that will help.'

And by and by, somewhat louder, he rehearsed them the same matter again, in other order and other words – so well and ornately, and nevertheless so evidently and plain, with voice, gesture and countenance so comely and so convenient – that every man much marvelled that heard him, and thought that they never had in their lives heard so evil a tale so well told. But were it for wonder or fear, or that each look that other should speak first, not one word was there answered of all the people that stood before, but all was as still as the midnight – not so much as rowning among them by which they might seem to commune what was best to do.

When the Mayor saw this, he with other partners of that counsel drew about the Duke and said that the people had not been accustomed there to be spoken to but by the recorder[65], which is the mouth of the city, and haply to him they will answer. With that, the recorder, called Fitzwilliam[66] – a sad man and an honest, which was so new come into that office that he never had spoken to the people before, and loath was with that matter to begin – notwithstanding, thereunto commanded by the Mayor, made rehearsal to the commons of that the Duke had twice rehearsed them himself. But the recorder so tempered his tale that he showed everything as the Duke's words and no part of his own. But all this nothing no change made in the people, which always after one stood as they had been men amazed. Whereupon the Duke rowned to the Mayer and said, 'This is a marvellous obstinate silence,' and therewith he turned to the people again with these words:

'Dear friends, we come to move you to that thing which peradventure we not so greatly needed, but that the lords of this realm and the commons of other parties might have sufficed, saving that we such love bear you, and so much set by you, that we would not gladly do without you that thing in which to be partners is your weal and honour, which, as it seems, either you see not or weigh not. Wherefore we require you give answer one or other: whether you be minded, as all the nobles of the realm be, to have this noble Prince, now Protector, to be your king or not.'

At these words the people began to whisper among

74

themselves secretly, that the voice was neither loud nor distinct, but as it were the sound of a swarm of bees; till at the last, in the nether end of the hall, a bushment of the Duke's servants – and Nesfield's[67], and other longing to the Protector, with some prentices and lads that thrust into the hall among the press – began suddenly at men's backs to cry out as loud as their throats would give, 'King Richard! King Richard!', and threw up their caps in token of joy. And they that stood before cast back their heads, marvelling thereof, but nothing they said. And when the Duke and the Mayor saw this manner, they wisely turned it to their purpose and said it was a goodly cry and a joyful to hear, every man with one voice, no man saying nay.

'Wherefore friends,' quod the Duke, 'since that we perceive it is all your whole minds to have this noble man for your king – whereof we shall make His Grace so effectual report that we doubt not but it shall redound to your great weal and commodity – we require you that you tomorrow go with us and we with you to His Noble Grace, to make our humble request to him in manner before remembered.'

And therewith the lords came down and the company dissolved and departed, the more part all sad, some with glad semblance that were not very merry; and some of those that came thither with the Duke, not able to dissemble their sorrow, were fain at his back to turn their face to the wall, while the dolour of their heart brast out at their eyes.

Then on the morrow after, the Mayor with all the aldermen and chief commoners of the city, in their best manner apparelled, assembling themselves together, resorted to Baynard's Castle[68] where the Protector lay. To which place repaired also, according to their appointment, the Duke of

Buckingham, with divers noblemen with him, beside many knights and other gentlemen. And thereupon the Duke sent word to the Lord Protector of the being there of a great and honourable company to move a great matter to His Grace. Whereupon the Protector made difficulty to come out to them, but if he first knew some part of their errand, as though he doubted and partly distrusted the coming of such number to him so suddenly without any warning or knowledge whether they came for good or harm.

Then the Duke, when he had shown this to the Mayor and other that they might thereby see how little the Protector looked for this matter, they sent to him by the messenger such loving message again, and therewith so humbly besought him to vouchsafe that they might resort to his presence to purpose their intent, of which they would to no other person any part disclose, that at the last he came forth of his chamber; and yet not down to them, but stood above in a gallery over them, where they might see him and speak to him, as though he would not yet come too near them till he wist what they meant. And thereupon the Duke of Buckingham first made humble petition to him, on the behalf of them all, that His Grace would pardon them, and license them to purpose to His Grace the intent of their coming without his displeasure – without which pardon obtained, they dared not be bold to move him of that matter. In which, albeit they meant as much honour to His Grace as wealth to all the realm beside, yet were they not sure how His Grace would take it, whom they would in no wise offend.

Then the Protector, as he was very gentle of himself, and also longed sore to wit what they meant, gave him leave to purpose what him liked – verily trusting, for the good mind that he bore them all, none of them anything would intend to him ward where with he ought to be grieved. When the Duke had this leave and pardon to speak, then waxed he bold to show him their intent and purpose, with all the causes moving them thereto as you before have heard; and finally to beseech His Grace that it would like him of his accustomed goodness and zeal to the realm, now with his eye of pity, to behold the long continued distress and decay of the same and to set his gracious hands to the redress and amendment thereof, by taking upon him the Crown and governance of this realm, according to his right and title lawfully descended to him; and to the laud of God, profit of the land, and to His Grace so much the more honour and less pain, in that never prince reigned upon any people that were so glad to live under his obeisance as the people of this realm under his.

When the Protector had heard the proposition, he looked very strangely thereat, and answered that all were it that he partly knew the things by them alleged to be true, yet such entire love he bore to King Edward and his children, that so much more regarded his honour in other realms about than the crown of any one, of which he was never desirous, that he could not find in his heart in this point to incline to their desire. For in all other nations where the truth were not well known, it should peradventure be thought that it were his own ambitious mind and device to depose the Prince and take himself the Crown – with which infamy he would not have his honour stained for any crown, in which he had ever perceived much more labour and pain than pleasure to him that so would so use it, as he that would not were not worthy to have it. Notwithstanding, he not only pardoned them the motion that they made him, but also thanked them for the love and hearty favour they bore him, praying them for his sake to give and bear the same to the Prince, under whom he was and would be content to live; and with his labour and counsel as far as should like the King to use him, he would do his uttermost devoir to set the realm in good state, which was already in this little while of his Protectorship (the praise given to God) well begun, in that the malice of such as were before of the contrary, and of new intended to be, were now – partly by good policy, partly more by God's special providence than man's provision – repressed.

Upon this answer given, the Duke, by the Protector's licence, a little rowned, as well with other noble men about him as with the Mayor and recorder of London. And after that upon like pardon desired and obtained, he showed aloud to the Protector that for a final conclusion that the realm was appointed King Edward's line should not any longer reign upon them, both for that they had so far gone that it was now no surety to retreat, as for that they thought it for the weal universal to take that way, although they had not yet begun it. Wherefore, if it would like His Grace to take the Crown upon him, they would humbly beseech him thereunto; if he would give them a resolute answer to the contrary, which they would be loath to hear, then must they needs seek and should not fail to find some other noble man that would.

These words much moved the Protector, which else, as every man may wit, would never of likelihood have inclined thereunto. But when he saw there was no other way, but that either he must take it or else he and his both go from it, he said to the lords and commons:

'Since we perceive well that all the realm is so set, whereof we be very sorry that they will not suffer in any wise King Edward's line to govern them, whom no man earthly can govern against their wills; and we well also perceive that no man is there to whom the Crown can by so just title appertain as to ourselves, as very right heir, lawfully begotten of the body of our most dear father Richard, late Duke of York – to which title is now joined your election, the nobles and commons of this realm, which we of all titles possible take for most effectual; we be content and agree favourably to incline to your petition and request, and according to the same, here we take upon us the royal estate, pre-eminence and kingdom of the two noble realms, England and France; the one from this day forward by us and our heirs to rule, govern and defend, the other by God's grace and your good help to get again and subdue, and establish for ever in due obedience to this realm of England, the advancement whereof we never ask of God longer to live than we intend to procure.'

With this there was a great shout, crying 'King Richard! King Richard!' And then the lords went up to the King (for so was he from that time called) and the people departed, talking diversely of the matter, every man as his fantasy gave him.

But much they talked and marvelled of the manner of this dealing that the matter was on both parts made so strange, as though neither had ever communed with other thereof before, when that themselves well wist there was no man so dull that heard them but he perceived well enough that all the matter was made between them. Howbeit, some excused that again and said all must be done in good order though. And men must sometimes for the manner sake not be aknowen what they know. For at the consecration of a bishop, every man wot well, by the paying for his bulls, that he purposes to be one, and though he pay for nothing else. And yet must he be twice asked whether he will be bishop or no, and he must twice say nay, and at the third time take it as compelled thereunto by his own will. And in a stage play all the people know right well that he that plays the sowdaine is percase a souter; yet if one should can so little good to show out of season what acquaintance he has with him, and call him by his own name while he stands in his majesty, one of his tormentors might hap to break his head, and worthy, for marring of the play. And so they said that these matters be kings' games, as it were stage plays, and for the more part played upon scaffolds, in which poor men be but the lookers-on – and they that wise be will meddle no further. For they that sometime step up and play with them, when they cannot play their parts, they disorder the play and do themselves no good.

The next day the Protector with a great train went to Westminster Hall and there, when he had placed himself in the Court of the King's Bench[69], declared to the audience that he would take upon him the Crown in that place there, where the king himself sits and ministers the law, because he considered that it was the chiefest duty of a king to minister the laws. Then, with as pleasant an oration as he could, he went about to win to him the nobles, the merchants, the artificers, and in conclusion all kind of men, but specially the lawyers of this realm. And finally, to the intent that no man should hate him for fear and that his deceitful clemency might get him the good-will of the people – when he had declared the discommodity of discord and the commodities of concord and unity – he made an open proclamation that he did put out of his mind all enmities, and that he there did openly pardon all offences committed against him. And to the intent that he might show a proof thereof, he commanded that one Fogge[70], whom he had long deadly hated, should be brought then before him. Who being brought out of the sanctuary by (for thither had he fled, for fear of him) in the sight of the people he took him by the hand. Which thing the common people rejoiced at and praised, but wise men took it for a vanity. In his return homeward, whomsoever he met, he saluted; for a mind that knows itself guilty, is in a manner dejected to a servile flattery.

When he had begun his reign, the twenty-sixth day of June, after this mockish election, then was he crowned the sixth day of July. And that solemnity was furnished for the most part with the selfsame provision that was appointed for the coronation of his nephew.

Now fell their mischief thick. And as the thing evil gotten is never well kept, through all the time of his reign never ceased there cruel death and slaughter, till his own destruction ended it. But as he finished his time with the best death, and the most righteous – that is to wit his own – so began he with the most piteous and wicked; I mean the lamentable murder of his innocent nephews, the young King and his tender brother, whose death and final infortune has nevertheless so far come in question that some remain yet in doubt whether they were in his days destroyed or no. Not for that only that Perkin Warbeck[71], by many folk's malice and more folk's folly so long space abusing the world, was as well with princes as the poorer people reputed and taken for the younger of those two; but for that also that all things were in late days so covertly demeaned, one thing pretended and another meant, that there was nothing so plain and openly proved, but that yet for the common custom of close and covert dealing, men had it ever inwardly suspect, as many well-counterfeited jewels make the true mistrusted. Howbeit, concerning that opinion, with the occasions moving either party, we shall have place more at large to entreat if we hereafter happen to write the time of the late noble Prince of famous memory, King Henry the Seventh, or percase that history of Perkin in any compendious process by itself.

But in the meantime, for this present matter, I shall rehearse you the dolorous end of those babes – not after every way that I have heard, but after that way they I have so heard by such men and by such means as methinks it were hard but it should be true.

King Richard, after his coronation, taking his way to Gloucester to visit in his new honour the town of which he bore the name of his old, devised, as he rode, to fulfil that thing which he before had intended. And forasmuch as his mind gave him that, his nephews living, men would not reckon that he could have right to the realm, he thought therefore without delay to rid them; as though the killing of his kinsmen could amend his cause and make him a kindly king. Whereupon he sent one John Green, whom he specially trusted, to Sir Robert Brackenbury, Constable of the Tower, with a letter and credence also that the same Sir Robert should in any wise put the two children to death. This John Green did his errand to Brackenbury, kneeling before Our Lady[72] in the Tower, who plainly answered that he would never put them to death, to die therefore; with which answer John Green, returning, recounted the same to King Richard at Warwick, yet in his way.

Wherewith he took such displeasure and thought, that the same night he said to a secret page of his, 'Ah, whom shall a man trust? Those that I have brought up myself, those that I had went would most surely serve me, even those fail me, and at my commandment will do nothing for me.'

'Sir,' quod his page, 'there lies one on your pallet without, that – I dare well say – to do Your Grace pleasure, the thing were right hard that he would refuse;' meaning this by Sir James Tyrell[73], which was a man of right goodly personage, and for nature's gifts worthy to have served a much better prince, if he had well served God and by grace obtained as much truth and goodwill as he had strength and wit. The man had an high heart and sore longed upward, not rising yet so fast as he had hoped, being hindered and kept under by the means of Sir Richard Radcliff and Sir William Catesby; which, longing for no more partners of the Prince's favour, and namely not for him whose pride they wist would bear no peer, kept him by secret drifts out of all secret trust. Which thing this page well had marked and known. Wherefore this occasion offered of very special friendship, he took his time to put him forward, and by such wise do him good, that all the enemies he had except the devil could never have done him so much hurt.

For upon this page's words King Richard arose (for this communication had he sitting at the draught, a convenient carpet for such a council) and came out into the pallet chamber, on which he found in bed Sir James and Sir Thomas Tyrell[74], of person like and brethren of blood, but nothing of kin in conditions. Then said the King merrily to them, 'What, sirs, be you in bed so soon?', and calling up Sir James broke to him secretly his mind in this mischievous matter, in which he found him nothing strange. Wherefore on the morrow he sent him to Brackenbury with a letter, by which he was commanded to deliver Sir James all the keys of the Tower for one night, to the end he might there accomplish the King's pleasure in such thing as he had given him commandment. After which letter delivered and the keys received, Sir James appointed the night next ensuing to destroy them, devising before and preparing the means.

The Prince, as soon as the Protector left that name and took himself as king, had it shown to him that he should not reign, but his uncle should have the Crown. At which word the

Prince, sore abashed, began to sigh and said, 'Alas, I would my uncle would let me have my life yet, though I lose my kingdom.' Then he that told him the tale used him with good words, and put him in the best comfort he could. But forthwith was the Prince and his brother both shut up, and all other removed from them, only one called Black Will or William Slaughter except, set to serve them and see them sure. After which time the Prince never tied his points, nor ought rought of himself, but with that young babe his brother lingered in thought and heaviness till this traitorous death delivered them of that wretchedness.

For Sir James Tyrell devised that they should be murdered in their beds. To the execution whereof he appointed Miles Forest, one of the four that kept them, a fellow fleshed in murder before time. To him he joined one John Dighton, his own horsekeeper, a big, broad, square, strong knave. Then, all the other being removed from them, this Miles Forest and John Dighton, about midnight – the sely children lying in their beds – came into the chamber and suddenly lapped them up among the clothes; so bewrapped them and entangled them, keeping down by force the featherbed and pillows hard to their mouths, that within a while, smored and stifled, their breath failing, they gave up to God their innocent souls into the joys of heaven, leaving to the tormentors their bodies dead in the bed. Which, after that the wretches perceived – first by the struggling with the pains of death, and after long lying still – to be thoroughly dead, they laid their bodies naked out upon the bed and fetched Sir James to see them. Which, upon the sight of them, caused those murderers to bury them at the stair foot, meetly deep in the ground, under a great heap of stones.

Then rode Sir James in great haste to King Richard, and showed him all the manner of the murder, who gave him great thanks, and, as some say, there made him knight. But he allowed not, as I have heard, the burying in so vile a corner, saying that he would have them buried in a better place, because they were a king's sons. Lo, the honourable courage of a king! Whereupon they say that a priest of Sir Robert Brackenbury took up the bodies again and secretly interred them in such place as, by the occasion of his death which only knew it, could never since come to light. Very truth is it and well known that at such time as Sir James Tyrell was in the Tower for treason committed against the most famous Prince, King Henry the Seventh,[75] both Dighton and he were examined and confessed the murder in manner above written; but whither the bodies were removed they could nothing tell.

And thus, as I have learnt of them that much knew and little cause had to lie, were these two noble princes – these innocent, tender children, born of most royal blood brought up in great wealth, likely long to live, to reign and rule in the realm – by traitorous tyranny taken, deprived of their estate, shortly shut up in prison, and privily slain and murdered; their bodies cast God wot where by the cruel ambition of their unnatural uncle and his dispiteous tormentors. Which things on every part well pondered, God never gave this world a more notable example, neither in what unsurety stands this worldly weal, or what mischief works the proud enterprise of an high heart, or finally what wretched end ensues such dispiteous cruelty.

For first to begin with the ministers, Miles Forest at St Martins piecemeal rotted away. Dighton, indeed, yet walks on alive in good possibility to be hanged before he die. But Sir James Tyrell died at Tower Hill, beheaded for treason. King Richard himself, as you shall hereafter hear, slain in the field, hacked and hewed of his enemies' hands, harried on horseback dead, his hair in despite torn and tugged like a cur-dog. And the mischief that he took, within less than three years of the mischief that he did; and yet all the meantime spent in much pain and trouble outward; much fear, anguish and sorrow within. For I have heard by credible report of such as were secret with his chamberers that, after this abominable deed done, he never had quiet in his mind; he never thought himself sure. Where he went abroad, his eyes whirled about, his body privily fenced, his hand ever on his dagger, his countenance and manner like one always ready to strike again. He took ill rest a-nights, lay long waking and musing, sore wearied with care and watch; rather slumbered than slept, troubled with fearful dreams, suddenly sometime start up, leapt out of his bed and run about the chamber. So was his restless heart continually tossed and tumbled with the tedious impression and stormy remembrance of his abominable deed.

Now had he outward no long time in rest. For hereupon soon after began the conspiracy, or rather good confederation, between the Duke of Buckingham and many other gentlemen against him.[76] The occasion whereupon the King and the Duke fell out is of divers folk divers wise pretended. This Duke, as I have for certain been informed, as soon as the Duke of Gloucester, upon the death of King Edward, came to York and there had solemn funeral service for King Edward, sent thither in the most secret wise he could one Percival, his trusty servant; who came in to John Ward, a chamberer of like secret trust with the Duke of Gloucester, desiring that in the most close and covert manner he might be admitted to the presence and speech of his master. And the Duke of Gloucester, advertised of his desire, caused him in the dead of the night, after all other folk avoided, to be brought to him in his secret chamber; where Percival, after his master's recommendation, showed him that he had secretly sent him to show him that in this new world he would take such part as he would, and wait upon him with a thousand good fellows if need were. The messenger, sent back with thanks and some secret instruction of the Protector's mind, yet met him again with further message from the Duke his master, within a few days after at Nottingham, whither the Protector from York with many gentlemen of the north country, to the number of six hundred horses, was come on his way to Londonward. And after secret meeting and communication had eftsoon departed.

Whereupon at Northampton the Duke met with the Protector himself with three hundred horses and from thence still continued with, partner of all his devices, till that after his coronation they departed as it seemed very great friends at Gloucester. From whence, as soon as the Duke came home, he so lightly turned from him and so highly conspired against him that a man would marvel whereof the change grew. And surely the occasion of their variance is of divers men diversely reported. Some have I heard say that the Duke, a little before the coronation, among other things required of the Protector the Duke of Hereford's lands, to which he pretended himself just inheritor. And forasmuch as the title which he claimed by inheritance was somewhat interlaced with the title to the Crown by the line of King Henry before deprived, the Protector conceived such indignation that he rejected the Duke's request with many spiteful and minatory words; which so wounded his heart with hatred and mistrust that he never after could endure to look aright on King Richard, but ever feared his own life – so far forth that when the Protector rode through London towards his coronation, he feigned himself sick because he would not ride with him. And the other, taking it in evil part, sent him word to rise and come ride, or he would make him be carried. Whereupon he rode on with evil will and that notwithstanding, on the morrow rose from the feast feigning himself sick; and King Richard said it was done in hatred and despite of him. And they say that ever after, continually, each of them lived in such hatred and distrust of other that the Duke verily looked to have been murdered at Gloucester – from which, nevertheless, he in fair manner departed.

But surely some right secret at the days[77] deny this. And many right wise men think it unlikely – the deep dissimuling nature of those both men considered, and what need in that green world the Protector had of the Duke, and in what peril the Duke stood if he fell once in suspicion of the tyrant – that either the Protector would give the Duke occasion of displeasure, or the Duke the Protector occasion of mistrust. And utterly men think that if King Richard had any such opinion conceived, he would never have suffered him to escape his hands. Very truth it is, the Duke was a high-minded man and evil could bear the glory of another, so that I have heard of some that said they saw it that the Duke, at such time as the crown was first set upon the Protector's head, his eye could not abide the sight thereof, but wried his head another way. But men say that he was of truth not well at ease, and that both to King Richard well known and not ill taken, nor any demand of the Duke's uncourteously rejected; but he both with great gifts and high behests in most loving, trusty manner departed at Gloucester.

But soon after his coming home to Brecknock, having there in his custody, by the commandment of King Richard, Dr Morton, Bishop of Ely – who as you before heard was taken in the council at the Tower – waxed with him familiar, whose wisdom abused his pride to his own deliverance and the Duke's destruction. The Bishop was a man of great natural wit, very well learned and honourable in behaviour, lacking no wise ways to win favour. He had been fast upon the part of King Henry while that part was in wealth, and nevertheless left it not, nor forsook it in woe; but fled the realm with the Queen and the Prince, while King Edward had the King in prison, never came home but to the field[78]. After which lost and that part utterly subdued, the other[79] for his fast faith and wisdom not only was content to receive him, but also wooed him to come, and had him from thenceforth both in secret trust and very special favour, which he nothing deceived. For he being, as you have heard, after King Edward's death first taken by the tyrant for his troth to the King, found the means to set this Duke in his top;[80] joined gentlemen together in aid of King Henry, devising first the marriage between him and King Edward's daughter, by which his faith declared and good service to both his masters at once, with infinite benefit to the realm, by the conjunction of those two bloods in one, whose several titles had long enquieted the land. He fled the realm, went to Rome, never minding more to meddle with the world till the noble Prince, King Henry the Seventh, got him home again, made him Archbishop of Canterbury and Chancellor of England; whereunto the Pope joined the honour of Cardinal. Thus, living many days in as much honour as one man might well wish, ended them so godly that his death, with God's mercy, well changed his life.

This man therefore, as I was about to tell you, by the long and often alternate proof, as well of prosperity as adverse fortune, had gotten by great experience (the very mother and mistress of wisdom) a deep insight in politic, worldly drifts; whereby, perceiving now this Duke glad to commune with him, fed him with fair words and many pleasant praises. And perceiving, by the process of their communications, the Duke's pride now and then baulk out a little breide of envy towards the glory of the King, and thereby feeling him easy to fall out if the matter were well handled, he craftily sought the ways to prick him forward, taking always the occasion of his coming, and so keeping himself close within his bonds that he rather seemed to follow him than to lead him. For when the Duke first began to praise and boast the King, and show how much profit the realm should take by his reign, my Lord Morton answered:

'Surely, My Lord, folly were it for me to lie, for if I would swear the contrary, Your Lordship would not, I ween, believe but that if the world would have gone as I would have wished, King Henry's son had had the Crown and not King Edward. But after that God had ordered him to lose it and King Edward to reign, I was never so mad that I would with a dead man strive against the quick. So was I to King Edward faithful chaplain, and glad would have been that his child had succeeded him. Howbeit, if the secret judgement of God have otherwise provided, I purpose not to spurn against a prick, nor labour to set up that God pulls down. And as for the late Protector, and now King…'

And even there he left, saying that he had already meddled too much with the world, and would from that day meddle with his book and his beads, and no further. Then longed the Duke sore to hear what he would have said – because he ended with the King and there so suddenly stopped – and exhorted him so familiarly between them twain to be so bold to say whatsoever he thought; whereof he faithfully promised there should never come hurt and peradventure more good than he would ween, and that himself intended to use his faithful, secret advice and counsel which, he said, was the only cause for which he procured of the King to have him in his custody where he might reckon himself at home, and else had he been put in the hands of them with whom he should not have founded the like favour.

The bishop right humbly thanked him and said, 'In good faith, My Lord, I love not much to talk much of princes, as thing not all out of peril, though the word be without fault; forasmuch as it shall not be taken as the party meant it, but as it pleases the Prince to construe it. And ever I think on Aesop's tale, that when the lion had proclaimed that on pain of death there should no horned beast abide in that wood, one that had in his forehead a bunch of flesh fled away a great pace. The fox that saw him run so fast asked him whither he made all that haste. And he answered, "In faith I neither wot nor reck, so I were once hence because of this proclamation made of horned beasts." "What fool," quod the fox, "you may abide well enough, the lion meant not by you, for it is no horn that is in your head." "No, marry," quod he, "that wot I well enough. But what and he call it a horn, where am I then?"'

The Duke laughed merrily at the tale, and said, 'My Lord, I warrant you, neither the lion nor the boar[81] shall pick any matter at anything here spoken, for it shall never come near their ear.'

'In good faith, sir,' said the Bishop, 'if it did, the thing that I was about to say, taken as well as afore God I meant it, could deserve but thank. And yet taken as I ween it would, might happen to turn me to little good and you to less.'

Then longed the Duke yet much more to wit what it was. Whereupon the Bishop said, 'In good faith, My Lord, as for the late Protector, since he is now king in possession, I purpose not to dispute his title. But for the weal of this realm, whereof His Grace has now the governance, and whereof I am myself one poor member, I was about to wish that to those good abilities whereof he has already right many little needing my praise, it might yet have pleased God for the better store to have given him some of such other excellent virtues meet for the rule of a realm, as our Lord has planted in the person of Your Grace.'

# NOTES

1. *The Chronicles of John Harding*, published in 1543, is the first place where More's *History* is known to have been printed; a slightly more accurate version was later printed in 1558 in Edward Hall's *Chronicle*.

2. This brief passage was written by William Rastell, More's nephew, who in 1557 published More's *History of Richard III* and his other writings in *The English Works*.

3. Despite More's claim, King Edward IV (1442–83) was in fact only forty years and eleven months old when he died.

4. Edward (1470–83), Prince of Wales and, for two months only, King Edward V.

5. Richard (*c*.1473–83), Duke of York.

6. Elizabeth of York (1466–1503) was crowned Queen to Henry VII in 1487.

7. Cecily (1469–1507) married three times.

8. Bridget (*c*.1480–*c*.1517) entered a convent in 1592.

9. Anne (1475–1511).

10. Katherine (1479–1517).

11. During a long power struggle between the Houses of York and Lancaster, Henry VI (1421–71) was deposed by Edward IV in 1461; he briefly regained the throne in 1470, but soon fell into Edward's hands, and died in the Tower of London in 1471.

12. More is overlooking the fact that Edward was still raising new taxes on the Scots.

13. Fifty thousand crowns annually.

14. Berwick Castle was captured from the Scots in 1482.

15. Richard (1452–85), Duke of Gloucester, was created Duke in 1461 when his brother Edward deposed Henry VI to become Edward IV; he went on to become Richard III through his notorious deeds.

16. Richard (1411–60), Duke of York, father of Edward IV and Richard III, claimed descent from Edward III via both his parents.

17. The Battle of Wakefield, 30th December 1460, when the claims on the monarchy of the House of York passed to Edward on the death of his father Richard, Duke of York.

18. Elizabeth Woodville (1437–92).

19. George (1449–78), Duke of Clarence, is thought to have accused the Queen of involvement in the death of his wife; this may have been the pretext for his brother Edward IV to see him off. He was secretly executed in the Tower.

20. These two men are thought to have been among Richard's servants, one an auditor, the other an attorney.

21. Thomas Grey (*c*.1456–*c*.1501), Lord Ferrers.

22. Lord Hastings (1431–83), a great support to Edward IV, was in fact called William, not Richard.

23. Anthony Woodville (*c*.1442–83).

24. The Duke of Buckingham (1454–83) was actually called Henry, not Edward. He had been pressured into marrying the Queen's sister, Catherine.

25. Richard Grey, second son from the Queen's first marriage.

26. Lord Rivers.

27. 'thus bore they folk in hand': *thus did they fool people.*

28. Sir Thomas Vaughan had been Chamberlain and Councillor to the young Prince Edward.

29. Pontefract

30. The right of taking sanctuary from one's enemies in a place of worship was derived from scripture; to breach someone's sanctuary was regarded as an offence against God.

31. Thomas Rotherham (1423–1500).

32. The great seal was the principal seal of the realm, used to authenticate signatures and documents of the highest importance.

33. Edward Shaa (d. 1487), Mayor of London.

34. John Russell (d. 1494); the actual transfer of the great seal took place the following month.

35. Thomas Bouchier (*c.*1404–86), Archbishop of Canterbury.

36. More means Canterbury, not York.

37. See note 36.

38. Exodus 21: 14 – 'But if a man schemes and kills another man deliberately, take him away from my altar and put him to death' (New International Version).

39. This is a reference to the two most important places of sanctuary in London: Westminster and St Martin Le Grand.

40. The Queen's brother, Lord Rivers, and son, Richard Grey, imprisoned by Richard, Duke of Gloucester.

41. In the changing fortunes and battle for power between the Houses of York and Lancaster during this period, the Queen's husband King Edward IV lost the throne for some months in 1470, returning after his enemies were defeated in 1471. The Queen took sanctuary at Westminister, where she gave birth to the heir to the throne.

42. Edward, Earl of Salisbury and Duke of Cornwall (1473–84).

43. William Catesby (*c.*1450–*c.*85) looked after Hastings' estates and business.

44. In fact the executions didn't take place until the end of June.

45. Jane Shore (*c.*1440–*c.*1527) wife of a mercer, had been a mistress of Edward IV.

46. Early editions of More's *History* have suggested that this was most likely to be Thomas Howard (d. 1524), Second Duke of Norfolk.

47. See note 44.

48. Edward Shaa's brother is thought have been called Ralph, not John.

49. Thomas Penker (d. *c.*1487).

50. Cecily, Duchess of York.

51. To Elizabeth Woodville in 1464.

52. Isabella (1451–1504), sister and adopted heir to Henry, King of Castilla.

53. Margaret of Anjou (1429–82).

54. Sir John Grey (1432–61); it is thought that the detail about Henry VI knighting him on the field is incorrect.

55. Edward IV had several illegitimate children.

56. In fact Edward's exile only lasted five months.

57. 14th April 1471.

58. The Court of Hustings was the highest tribunal for London.

59. Sir Thomas Burdet (1420–77) was said to have been executed for imprudently criticising the King over a trivial matter.

60. Sir John Markham (d. *c.*1479) resigned from office because of the treatment of Sir Thomas Cook (1420–78), a former Mayor of London who had been accused of high treason for lending money to Queen Margaret; Cook's lands and properties were pillaged while he was in prison.

61. See note 60.

62. See note 19.

63. 'there is of that House that now': *there is of that House [one man] that now.*

64. Solomon; the quote is from Ecclesiastes 10: 16.

65. The recorder was the assistant to the Mayor.

66. Sir Thomas Fitzwilliam (1427–97).

67. A lackey of Richard's.

68. Baynard's Castle was the residence of Richard's mother, Cecily, the Duchess of York.

69. The Court of the King's Bench was where the King heard pleas and made judgements.

70. Sir John Fogge (1425–90) had been the treasurer of Edward IV's household.

71. Perkin Warbeck (*c.*1474–99), of Flemish origin, was an imposter to the throne in later years, purporting to be the youngest of the two sons of Edward IV whom Richard had murdered in the Tower.

72. A statue of the Virgin Mary.

73. Sir James Tyrell (1445–1502).

74. Sir Thomas Tyrell (1450–1510), younger brother of James.

75. Sir James Tyrell was executed for treason in 1502.

76. The Duke of Buckingham's machinations against his former ally Richard ended in failure and execution in November 1483.

77. 'some right secret at the days': *those who were privy to secret matters at that time.*

78. 'field': *battle*, i.e. the Battle of Tewkesbury (1471).

79. Edward IV.

80. 'to set this Duke in his top': *to ruin this Duke.*

81. Richard III's coat of arms was formed by the lion and the boar.

a slope: *obliquely*

abused: *deceived*

adhibit: *admitted*

advertisement: *instruction*

after: *like*

aggrieve: *exaggerate*

allective: *enticement*

almoise: *a good deed*

alow: *below*

at erst: *for the first time*

atonement: *agreement*

bare him sore: *disliked him very much*

baste: *bastardy*

be aknowen: *acknowledge*

bend: *faction*

bigamy: *marriage to a widow*

brast: *burst*

breide: *outburst*

briginders: *body armour*

bushment: *group*

but if: *unless*

can so little good: *be so foolish*

can: *know*

careful: *full of care,* i.e. *full of grief*

cast: *trick*

certes: *certainly*

chamberer: *valet*

chance: *case*

close: *cloistered*

cognisaunce: *coat of arms*

colourable: *fake*

commodity: *advantage*

compass: *scheme*

conditions: *morals*

convenient: *appropriate*

could: *could; know*

could his good: *knew what was good for him*

coumpinable: *friendly*

courage: *nature*

cunning: *learned*

debonair: *gracious*

demean: *rule; treat*

despite: *contempt*

devolute: *passed down*

discommodity: *disadvantage*

draught: *toilet*

drift: *scheming; scheme*

eftsoons: *for the second time; soon after*

encheason: *reason*

enemious: *hostile*

enquieted: *disturbed*

ensured: *betrothed*

erst: *first*

evil: *ill; unskilled*

fame: *talk; rumour*

farder: *afraid*
favour: *appearance*
fenced: *armoured*
field: *battle*
fleshed: *blooded; initiated*
flockmeal: *in groups*
for that: *because*
for the manner sake: *for the sake of appearances*
forced: *cared*
forestudied: *anticipated*
fortherly: *favourable*
froward: *perverse; awkward*
gaincalled: *brought back again*
gay: *unimportant*
gloss: *pretext*
goodly towardness: *aptitude*
grennes: *snares*
groundly: *thoroughly*
haply: *perhaps*
hardly: *by all means*
harness: *armour*
hawsed: *raised*
heart brenning: *jealousy*
homely: *rough*
horsebackward: *ready to ride*
hoverly: *expedient*
importable: *unbearable*
in manner desolate: *almost solitary*
in manner: *as it were*

in the wight: *to blame*
in ure: *habituated*
incontinent: *immediately*
indifferently: *impartially*
indited: *composed*
infortune: *misfortune*
it booted not: *it had no effect*
kindly: *naturally*
leger: *slight*
let: *hindrance*
letting: *hesitating; hindering*
lever: *rather*
lief: *beloved*
light adown: *dismounted*
list: *pleased*
look me: *see*
look: *expect*
made so strange: *presented as though spontaneous*
maistry: *achievement*
mannequellers: *murderers*
maugry: *despite*
mind: *plan*
minister: *provide*
nought: *naught*
needs cost: *necessarily*
occasion: *action*
of estate convenient: *of suitable rank*
on a roar: *into confusion*
percase: *perchance*
pill: *pillage*

plight: *condition*
points: *cords for lacing garments*
port: *bearing*
pretended: *reported*
prevent: *act before*
process: *narrative*
provision: *foresight*
puissaunce: *armed force*
quailed: *impeded*
recidivation: *relapse*
resort: *company of people*
rivelled: *wrinkled*
rooms: *stations; offices*
rought: *cared*
rowning: *whispering*
rud: *red*
sad: *mature; serious; grave*
sample: *example*
secret: *intimate*
self: *self; same*
sely: *innocent*
several: *separate*
shift: *deal*
slipper: *unstable*
smored: *smothered*
sounded: *gave rise*
sowdaine: *sultan*
spialles: *spies*
standing: *considering*
stately of stomach: *haughty*
states: *noblemen*

strange: *sparing*
strengths: *strongholds*
sure: *betrothed*
tenders: *esteems*
to a field: *to battle*
to horsebackward: *towards horseback*, i.e. *ready to ride*
to spurn against a prick: *to resist it*
trains: *traps*
trusses: *packs*
tuition: *guardianship; protection*
unsitting: *unbecoming*
unthrifts: *spendthrifts*
ure: *see* in ure
wast: *knew*
ween: *think; suppose*
werish: *shrivelled*
whole: *as one*
wight: *blame*
will: *justification*
wist: *knew*
without colour: *without evidence*
worth: *become*
worthy: *rightly*
wot: *knew*
wried: *twisted*

Thomas More was born on 7th February 1478 (or 1477, according to some sources) in London. He was the son of Sir John More, a prominent barrister. At the age of thirteen he was placed in the household of Cardinal Morton, the Archbishop of Canterbury, who was sufficiently impressed by the boy to send him to Oxford from around 1492. There he studied Greek, Latin, French, History and Mathematics. Returning to London two years later, he studied Law at Lincoln's Inn, where he was later called to the Bar and made a bencher.

More also made the acquaintance of scholars – in 1497 he was introduced to Erasmus, who became his life-long friend. He read theology, and delivered lectures on Augustine. He considered joining the priesthood at this time, and although he ultimately declined this path, he would retain such monastic habits as penitence and fasting throughout his life.

Having turned aside from the priesthood, More devoted himself to civil matters. After being elected a Member of Parliament, he immediately urged a decrease in Henry VII's proposed appropriation of his subjects' wealth. As a result, the King's income was reduced to a third of the original amount, and Henry VII retaliated against More by imprisoning his father in the Tower until a fine was paid, and Thomas retired from public life. He married in 1505, and had four children with his wife, who died in 1511. He remarried soon after.

After the death of Henry VII in 1509, and the coronation of Henry VIII, More began to find favour in public life again. In 1514 he was chosen by Cardinal Wolsey as a member of an embassy to Flanders. It was during this journey that he began the literary work for which he is most famous, *Utopia*, published in 1516. In 1521 he was knighted and made sub-treasurer to the King. He garnered Henry VIII's favour at this time, and helped him to write a repudiation of Luther. In 1523 he was elected Speaker of the House of Commons.

In 1529 More succeeded Wolsey as Lord Chancellor, a position never before held by a layman. He proved a brilliant judge, exhausting the case log for the only time in English history. However, conflict arose in his relationship with the monarch from his opposition to the King's positions on divorce, papal supremacy, and laws against heretics. He also disagreed with the King's self-appointment as Head of the Church. This led him to resign his Lord Chancellorship in 1532.

On 14th April 1534, More refused to swear an oath supporting the Act of Succession, for which he was taken into custody. He was indicted for high treason on 1st July 1535, and beheaded on Tower Hill on 6th July. He was canonised by Pope Pius XI in 1935.

## HESPERUS PRESS CLASSICS

Hesperus Press, as suggested by the Latin motto, is committed to bringing near what is far – far both in space and time. Works written by the greatest authors, and unjustly neglected or simply little known in the English-speaking world, are made accessible through new translations and a completely fresh editorial approach. Through these classic works, the reader is introduced to the greatest writers from all times and all cultures.

For more information on Hesperus Press, please visit our website: **www.hesperuspress.com**

ET REMOTISSIMA PROPE

# SELECTED TITLES FROM HESPERUS PRESS

| Joseph Conrad | *The Return* | Colm Tóibín |
| Gabriele D'Annunzio | *The Book of the Virgins* | Tim Parks |
| Dante Alighieri | *The Divine Comedy: Inferno* | |
| Dante Alighieri | *New Life* | Louis de Bernières |
| Daniel Defoe | *The King of Pirates* | Peter Ackroyd |
| Marquis de Sade | *Incest* | Janet Street-Porter |
| Charles Dickens | *The Haunted House* | Peter Ackroyd |
| Charles Dickens | *A House to Let* | |
| Fyodor Dostoevsky | *The Double* | Jeremy Dyson |
| Fyodor Dostoevsky | *Poor People* | Charlotte Hobson |
| Alexandre Dumas | *One Thousand and One Ghosts* | |
| Joseph von Eichendorff | *Life of a Good-for-nothing* | |
| George Eliot | *Amos Barton* | Matthew Sweet |
| Henry Fielding | *Jonathan Wild the Great* | Peter Ackroyd |
| F. Scott Fitzgerald | *The Popular Girl* | Helen Dunmore |
| F. Scott Fitzgerald | *The Rich Boy* | John Updike |
| Gustave Flaubert | *Memoirs of a Madman* | Germaine Greer |
| E.M. Forster | *Arctic Summer* | Anita Desai |
| Ugo Foscolo | *Last Letters of Jacopo Ortis* | Valerio Massimo Manfredi |
| Giuseppe Garibaldi | *My Life* | Tim Parks |
| Elizabeth Gaskell | *Lois the Witch* | Jenny Uglow |
| Théophile Gautier | *The Jinx* | Gilbert Adair |
| André Gide | *Theseus* | |
| Johann Wolfgang von Goethe | *The Man of Fifty* | A.S. Byatt |
| Nikolai Gogol | *The Squabble* | Patrick McCabe |
| Thomas Hardy | *Fellow-Townsmen* | Emma Tennant |
| L.P. Hartley | *Simonetta Perkins* | Margaret Drabble |
| Nathaniel Hawthorne | *Rappaccini's Daughter* | Simon Schama |
| E.T.A. Hoffmann | *Mademoiselle de Scudéri* | Gilbert Adair |
| Victor Hugo | *The Last Day of a Condemned Man* | Libby Purves |

| | | |
|---|---|---|
| Aldous Huxley | *After the Fireworks* | Fay Weldon |
| Joris-Karl Huysmans | *With the Flow* | Simon Callow |
| Henry James | *In the Cage* | Libby Purves |
| Franz Kafka | *Metamorphosis* | Martin Jarvis |
| Franz Kafka | *The Trial* | Zadie Smith |
| John Keats | *Fugitive Poems* | Andrew Motion |
| Heinrich von Kleist | *The Marquise of O–* | Andrew Miller |
| D.H. Lawrence | *Daughters of the Vicar* | Anita Desai |
| D.H. Lawrence | *The Fox* | Doris Lessing |
| Leonardo da Vinci | *Prophecies* | Eraldo Affinati |
| Giacomo Leopardi | *Thoughts* | Edoardo Albinati |
| Mikhail Lermontov | *A Hero of Our Time* | Doris Lessing |
| Nikolai Leskov | *Lady Macbeth of Mtsensk* | Gilbert Adair |
| Carlo Levi | *Words are Stones* | Anita Desai |
| Jack London | *Before Adam* | |
| Niccolò Machiavelli | *Life of Castruccio Castracani* | Richard Overy |
| Xavier de Maistre | *A Journey Around my Room* | Alain de Botton |
| André Malraux | *The Way of the Kings* | Rachel Seiffert |
| Katherine Mansfield | *In a German Pension* | Linda Grant |
| Katherine Mansfield | *Prelude* | William Boyd |
| Edgar Lee Masters | *Spoon River Anthology* | Shena Mackay |
| Guy de Maupassant | *Butterball* | Germaine Greer |
| Lorenzino de' Medici | *Apology for a Murder* | Tim Parks |
| Herman Melville | *The Enchanted Isles* | Margaret Drabble |
| Prosper Mérimée | *Carmen* | Philip Pullman |
| Sándor Pëtofi | *John the Valiant* | George Szirtes |
| Francis Petrarch | *My Secret Book* | Germaine Greer |
| Luigi Pirandello | *Loveless Love* | |
| Edgar Allan Poe | *Eureka* | Sir Patrick Moore |
| Alexander Pope | *The Rape of the Lock and A Key to the Lock* | Peter Ackroyd |

| | | |
|---|---|---|
| Alexander Pope | *Scriblerus* | Peter Ackroyd |
| Antoine-François Prévost | *Manon Lescaut* | Germaine Greer |
| Marcel Proust | *Pleasures and Days* | A.N. Wilson |
| Alexander Pushkin | *Dubrovsky* | Patrick Neate |
| Alexander Pushkin | *Ruslan and Lyudmila* | Colm Tóibín |
| François Rabelais | *Pantagruel* | Paul Bailey |
| François Rabelais | *Gargantua* | Paul Bailey |
| Christina Rossetti | *Commonplace* | Andrew Motion |
| George Sand | *The Devil's Pool* | Victoria Glendinning |
| Jean-Paul Sartre | *The Wall* | Justin Cartwright |
| Friedrich von Schiller | *The Ghost-seer* | Martin Jarvis |
| Mary Shelley | *Transformation* | |
| Percy Bysshe Shelley | *Zastrozzi* | Germaine Greer |
| Stendhal | *Memoirs of an Egotist* | Doris Lessing |
| Robert Louis Stevenson | *Dr Jekyll and Mr Hyde* | Helen Dunmore |
| Theodor Storm | *The Lake of the Bees* | Alan Sillitoe |
| Italo Svevo | *A Perfect Hoax* | Tim Parks |
| Jonathan Swift | *Directions to Servants* | Colm Tóibín |
| W.M. Thackeray | *Rebecca and Rowena* | Matthew Sweet |
| Leo Tolstoy | *The Death of Ivan Ilych* | |
| Leo Tolstoy | *Hadji Murat* | Colm Tóibín |
| Ivan Turgenev | *Faust* | Simon Callow |
| Mark Twain | *The Diary of Adam and Eve* | John Updike |
| Mark Twain | *Tom Sawyer, Detective* | |
| Giovanni Verga | *Life in the Country* | Paul Bailey |
| Jules Verne | *A Fantasy of Dr Ox* | Gilbert Adair |
| Edith Wharton | *The Touchstone* | Salley Vickers |
| Oscar Wilde | *The Portrait of Mr W.H.* | Peter Ackroyd |
| Virginia Woolf | *Carlyle's House and Other Sketches* | Doris Lessing |
| Virginia Woolf | *Monday or Tuesday* | Scarlett Thomas |
| Emile Zola | *For a Night of Love* | A.N. Wilson |